Bills of Materials

The Dow Jones-Irwin/APICS
Series in Production Management

Supported by the American Production
and Inventory Control Society

Bills of Materials

Hal Mather, CFPIM

DOW JONES-IRWIN
Homewood, Illinois   60430

ISBN 0-87094-947-0

Library of Congress Catalog Card No. 86-71398

Printed in the United States of America

1 2 3 4 5 6 7 8 9 0   K   4 3 2 1 0 9 8 7

Preface

Even though Bills of Materials are a key part of the data in all manufacturing companies, there is very little written about them. I presume because we have always had them, no-one felt them worthwhile to write about. But the roles assigned to Bills of Materials have changed dramatically in the past 20 years. The traditional uses have expanded ever since formal manufacturing control systems started to be developed. And this has led to real conflicts between the traditional users and the new applications. I have attempted to sort out some of these conflicts and show how all groups can get what they want from a well thought out Bill of Material system.

The subject goes much deeper than just the Bill of Material, though. Often the design of products can be shown, through the new uses of Bills of Materials, to be inadequate in todays competitive world. New, formal manufacturing control systems have focused our attention on the Master Production Schedule and our need to predict the future as accurately as possible. But many Bills of Materials were not thought out with this requirement, neither were many products designed for it either. But there's no point in designing a better mousetrap if you can't predict how many of which version a customer will buy sometime in the future. From a business point of view, you'll either have too much inventory to support the sales or customers will be clamoring for a product you can't deliver with a competitive lead time. So the design of many products and the structure of their Bills of Materials go hand in hand to meet the need for "accurate" forecasts.

The whole management of Bills of Materials needs reevaluating in most companies. This document has evolved from a hand written instruction, frequently combined with the pictorial view of the product, into the backbone set of data for a business. Product costs, factory schedules, materials and purchased parts procurement, customer delivery promises, sales prices, and much more are often generated through a modern Bill of Material system. The controls on access, maintenance and integrity of this data are orders of magnitude higher under the latter scenario than the old, manual methods.

We need to develop additional skills and management processes to handle this more demanding condition, which is a weak spot in many companies today. A clear understanding of responsibilities and organization will help to show where these changes are needed.

As with all actions that are taken in a business, you have to ask, "What's in it for me?" From the top manager's perspective, improved customer service, lower inventories and more reliable information. For middle managers, data structured so they can use it to perform their functions more effectively. For people within the organization who use Bills of Materials, less frustration in fighting City Hall and the morale boosting experience of working on a team to beat competition. I am sure the rewards will exceed the costs. The only question is, "When will you get started?"

Hal Mather.

Acknowledgements

Every author of a technical book owes a lot of his ideas to people who helped him develop his thoughts. I am no exception. Articles and books published by others, lectures I have attended, as well as informal discussions have all helped to develop the material in this book.

Some key names stand out in this development. Joe Orlicky with his book *Material Requirements Planning,* Dick Bourke with his book *Bills of Materials, the Key Building Block,* Dave Garwood with his article *Stop: Before You Use the Bill Processor,* and numerous publications by IBM. But the man with most influence on the development of my thoughts is my long time associate and good friend, George Plossl. His writings and teachings, always so clear and concise, have done most to clarify my thoughts.

On the publication side I want to thank my wife, Jean, for giving up a large part of our vacations in the past 18 months to writing. Her patience in typing and retyping the manuscript was stretched to the limit but luckily it held. Thanks also to Yvonne Wright, for her editorial changes that make the book much more readable, and to her husband, Jim Wright for actually getting the book to press.

—Hal Mather.

CONTENTS

1 The Pressure for Change

Bills of materials, recipes and formulations are terms used to describe the documents that define how a product is made. These documents, whether in physical form or simply a mental image, have been used by manufacturers since manufacturing began. Recently, however, this data has taken on more uses than the traditional one of defining the product so it can be made. The ever increasing pressure on companies to be more productive, react faster to marketplace changes, and do this with lower and lower inventories, has demanded and is still demanding significant changes to the traditional ways of managing a manufacturing business.

The most significant change has been the frequent use of computers in planning and control systems. Bills of materials are a key set of information in these formal systems. They are used by all parts of the organization and have recently been subjected to conflicting pressures from various organizational groups who want them to suit their needs and their systems. Design engineers, the traditional custodians of this information, are caught in the middle trying to appease the various factions with compromises none accept. And frequently, out of desperation, they decide to make them suit *their* needs, which at least are well defined.

An especially significant factor is the use of computers for storage, manipulation and retrieval of the bills of materials. Prior to this, data was maintained and sometimes modified by each organizational function to suit their own limited needs. With the computer on the scene, though, the concept of one common set of data that serves all users has evolved. This has occurred for a variety of reasons: less maintenance, more accurate data with only one set of numbers, and less stored information. This change served to make the conflicts worse because then the specific needs of one function affected all others.

But the major changes to bills of materials and how they are structured come and will continue to come from advancements in the state-of-the-art within manufacturing control systems. These systems are the logistical planning arm of a manufacturer, creating material procurement plans and schedules for the factory to support future product sales. As improvements in this planning process have the potential to simultaneously improve customer service, increase productivity, and reduce inventories, they have received a lot of attention. The development of techniques in this area since the mid 1960's has been dramatic, mostly tied to the power of computers to quickly process large amounts of data. As material procurement and factory schedules are predicated on the product definition, bills of materials have figured prominently in these advancements.

Additional pressures are coming. The day of the automated hard goods factory is not too distant, where huge capital expenditures for machinery will allow products to be made attended only by technicians concerned with keeping the machinery operating at peak efficiency. This is already a reality in the process industry, for example, oil refineries and breweries. It will become a reality for hard goods manufacture because of the shortage of skilled workers and the need to combat excessive wage increases. But in an automated environment, having the right materials at the right time and scheduling the plant correctly will be of vital importance because of the huge cost penalties of idle machinery.

Another pressure in most plants is the cost of transportation, rising from a virtually insignificant part of a product's cost a few years ago to a larger and larger percentage. As energy costs continue to escalate faster than inflation and as transportation fuels become more subject to interrupted supply, the trend will be to smaller plants strategically located near regional markets. This is already true in some industries, for example car battery manufacturers, where the costs of transportation have traditionally been high because of the weight involved. The challenge will be to make small plants efficient and profitable while they produce a wide variety of products in low volume. Part of the solution resides in product design changes and development of bills of materials suited to this environment.

The manufacturing control system of a company depends on a future prediction of the products customers might buy. Few companies procure all materials and schedule their plants based only on known customer's orders. But predicting the future sales of a business is one of the most difficult jobs for manufacturers. The product design and bill of material structure can make a large contribution in aiding the forecasting process. The technique that uses this prediction, by considering booked orders and/or forecasts, is called Master Production Scheduling. The master production schedule will not be described here in detail, as some excellent books and articles already exist on this subject. However, certain key elements of the master production schedule will be presented because of their direct impact on the structure of bills of materials.

In retrospect, manufacturing control systems have been developed backwards. When computers were installed in plants, bills of materials that had been available for a long time, describing the product for engineers and manufacturing people, were loaded into the computer with little consideration of the end uses for this information. As soon as it was realized bills of materials provided the framework for all procurement and scheduling activities, it was also obvious that a master production schedule was needed. Many people then tried to predict the future based on the old, traditional bills of materials resident within the computer system. Just like the man who swallowed his contact lenses, we now have 20/20 hindsight which shows this was the wrong approach.

What should have happened was serious consideration of the best way for companies to generate the best master production schedule. Only after this was defined should bills of materials have been developed, not only to support all traditional uses but primarily to support the master production schedule. The backwards approach taken has caused a significant waste of resources by companies now actively changing their bills of materials from traditional formats to ones more conducive to supporting a valid master production schedule.

A variety of bills of materials formats are available to assist in making a good master production schedule. The selection will depend, among other things, upon the specific product design. This new role for bills of materials to support not only all functional areas but also to serve as a key ingredient of the planning and control systems of every manufacturer, gives it the potential to affect significantly a company's financial performance for better or worse.

Uses

Bills of materials have a wide variety of uses, depending on the function using them. Each use puts different demands on the data, so all uses must be clearly understood before one bill of materials can be constructed to suit all these demands. Some of the more common uses for bills of materials follow.

Product Definition. Bills of materials must specify the ingredients used to make a product. This is the major role engineering departments assign to this data. The product must be described so there are no misunderstandings about the product make-up. Many times this definition must be approved by regulatory agencies such as standards setting boards, independent testing laboratories, or governmental agencies. Bills of materials then form a key part of the documentation submitted to these agencies for approval before the product can be sold on the open market.

Manufacturing instructions. Sometimes bills of materials form part of the instructions for manufacturing a product. An example is a company making an assembled product, where the organization of items on their bills of materials is in the normal assembly sequence. Frequently, when the bills of materials are created this way, there is no need for a final assembly drawing for finished products; the bills of materials sequence eliminates the need for a pictorial display.

Engineering change control. Bills of materials have to be maintained accurately. This maintenance is sometimes needed to correct errors on the original document, but can also be a result of product performance improvements, cost reductions, or the incorporation of additional features. Implementation of such changes must consider phase-out of the old product, introduction of the new, and could possibly include announcements to the marketplace. This change control is especially critical for companies where revised approvals from regulatory agencies are necessary for the new design. The Food and Drug Administration, as well as the military, are good examples of agencies where tight control over the implementation of changes to a product approved earlier is managed with extreme caution. Bills of materials have to handle the transition from the old design to the new and in many cases help record when the change occurred. Logging such things as the serial numbers of the last old and first new unit produced, the lot number when the change was introduced, or simply the date, can be part of this activity.

Service parts support. Most products today are highly reliable. However, when parts break or wear out, the replacement parts necessary to fix the failure must be delivered to the broken unit quickly. Good examples are automobiles or home appliances. On the industrial scene, every piece of productive machinery made must be well supported with spare parts to keep these units functioning efficiently during their expected life.

Bills of materials can be a convenient device to record a product's definition at the time it is built. This may be several revisions earlier than today's current production models so retention of the configuration when particular units were built is critical. This is especially true for products unique to a customer, for example telephone exchanges or computers, where it is necessary to keep track of a specific customer's revision level of product, even considering changes retroactively fitted to units in the field. This is because later changes have to interface correctly with each specific configuration of installed product.

Liability/warranty protection. The large claims collected by people injured by products and today's emphasis on product liability require the product definition at the time of sale to form part of the defense against any such liability suit for a company. As bills of materials define the product they have to perform this function. Along with liability problems are warranty problems. Significant escalation in warranty claims for a product should be traceable directly to a revision level in the bills of materials. The changes made at that time can be reevaluated to determine the problem and find a solution. Similarly, if a change has been implemented to reduce warranty costs, its success can also be checked through the bill of materials history file and claims by serial or model number from the field.

Planning material procurement and scheduling the plant. Bills of materials define what materials are needed from vendors and what items must be made in the plant to produce a product. The specific location of these items within the bills of materials structure, combined with the time estimates for completion of each task, provide the needed timing of material procurement and schedules for manufacturing. Material requirements planning is the technique used for this planning and scheduling activity.

The use of bills of materials for planning and scheduling is the single largest reason for their change. Traditional ways of defining products do not consider the need for and problems of predicting the future well. Without this future prediction it is impossible to create a valid master production schedule. And without this, material procurement and factory schedules can only be based on past history—rarely valid in today's dynamically changing world. Poor customer service, inflated inventories and poor productivity are the result.

Because of the serious implications that bill of material structures have on a company's ability to compete, both material requirements planning and the master production schedule will be covered in greater detail in Chapter 5.

Order entry facility. Many products consist of a variety of options selectable by customers to configure a product unique to their needs, for example, automobiles or machine tools. Because of the huge variety of unique end products that can be built through the selection of options, the order entry procedure frequently configures the end product bill of materials. For example, when specifying a custom built automobile, selection of the basic family such as Cadillac Fleetwood, defines the chassis and a few other common components. Selection of a specific engine size, transmission type, body style, seat configuration, or any of the other options is done through an order entry check-off list which creates the bill of materials for the final product. This suggests that bills of materials in this environment should never be complete to the end product level but should be sub-groupings of parts that define the options. The end product is then configured through the order entry program. Fortunately, the bills of materials needed to configure a finished product through the order entry cycle are frequently the same as those needed to help predict the future and hence create a valid master production schedule.

The technique of selecting and defining end products through an order entry cycle is called "menu selection", similar to the way a waitress or waiter easily specifies a uniquely configured meal for the individual tastes of people in a restaurant from a limited variety of options. Without this facility a restaurant menu would be a book about 3 inches thick. One part number would define a specific meal, such as type of juice, appetizer, salad, main course, dessert, and beverage. A different part number would define the identical meal except for a change in one of the options. You would then order by number, perhaps taking up to an hour to find your specific needs listed. And woe betide anyone who wants to make a substitution as that would mean changing the kitchen instructions also, with attendant chance of error.

This facility of using a computer to configure a finished product to a given customer's need is not used by enough companies. The penalty is a smaller product offering with large engineering staffs maintaining end product configurations. A significant opportunity for simultaneously improving customer service and reducing inventories is available to these companies. It does require a higher level of engineering expertise and much more thought about the options possibility when new products are being designed, but the benefits can be significant.

Pick or kit lists. When manufacturing a product from many components or ingredients, a list of parts or materials to be withdrawn from the stocking location prior to the manufacturing process is often needed. This is especially true for pharmaceutical manufacture where tight control is exercised over the the actual dispensing of chemicals to the manufacturing process to ensure meeting product specifications.

Many times, especially in large assembly operations, the instructions for the withdrawal of parts from inventory must not only state the quantity needed for the planned production but must also say where in the plant to deliver this material. For very long assembly times, such as those needed for power generation equipment, the picking instructions must also be timed to suit stages of the assembly cycle.

The issuance of materials to a batch of product being made must often by identified to a specific lot number for the batch. This is mandatory for the food and pharmaceutical industries where product problems found in the field can be hazardous to human health. If problems are found, it must be possible to trace the manufacturing lot back to all its ingredients. Hence the pick list forms a key part of the lot number traceability program.

Scarce material or resource analysis. Whenever materials are in short supply, the problem is what products can or should be made with the available materials. To solve the problem requires an ability to "implode" or trace upwards through the bill of materials to find the end items using this material. A "where used" list is a bill of materials re-sorted, showing a component and all the parent items that use it. This need to "climb up" bills of materials must be considered when configuring the data and deciding on the method of storage.

Costing. Bills of materials form the nucleus of a product costing program. Combining the cost of materials necessary to produce a product with the conversion or labor costs provides an accurate picture of the product's total cost. Many times, however, accurate costing can occur without a full definition of the product. An example is identical items painted a variety of colors but where the costs of different color paints and the labor involved are identical. In this case, costing the products can be done regardless of the end item part number.

Sometimes low cost, purchased items are expensed when received from vendors and their value becomes part of the overhead or burden rate for the factory. Hence their inclusion or omission from bills of materials is not important from a costing standpoint. An example is wire used for connecting electrical components but bought in bulk rolls and issued to the factory on an "as needed" basis. Another example is hardware, often issued to the factory floor in bulk amounts and ignored from a costing standpoint.

The other side of the coin, though, is the need to cost products as accurately as possible to provide good margin and profitability analysis. Sometimes this demands additional items and quantities be listed on bills of materials that are not traditionally present, for example welding rods, grease and paint. Recent pressures on the accounting profession for product line profitability reporting will increase the amount of detail contained within bills of materials for more complete and accurate costing.

Pricing. Bills of materials can be used to price products sold to customers. This is especially true for products made from options. The order entry technique which configures the end product must provide this facility.

Backflushing. The term "backflushing" is the common name for the technique more correctly called "reverse explosion." It is a method of relieving on-hand inventories of components and raw materials used in a manufacturing process. When a quantity of a given product is finished and reported complete, the reported quantity is extended by the quantity per unit of all components or ingredients in this product's bill of materials. This calculates, for all the items in the bill of materials, the theoretical amounts that were consumed.

These theoretical amounts are then subtracted from the on-hand or work-in-process inventories for each item to give the true balance remaining. The need for picking and issuing parts or materials to a specific factory order is eliminated, giving a signficant reduction in paperwork transactions.

Sometimes backflushing is used to relieve inventories at each operational step in the manufacturing process. In this case, the bill of materials must either be structured to suit operational relief, or each item in the bill of materials must be coded to a specific operational step in the process.

It is difficult to get and maintain accurate inventory records with backflushing. Errors in reporting the quantity or time identity of the item produced, as well as bill of materials errors, are processed into the inventory system automatically. Unreported substitutions, scrap, or floor losses are not considered and cannot be caught by the inventory system.

Of course, the alternative of issuing parts and materials to a discrete work order is not always possible, so backflushing has to be used. A good example is the consumption of bulk materials drawn from a silo or bulk container directly into the manufacturing process. Flow meters are often not accurate, especially when moving powders or slurries.

For repetitive manufacturers, there are no discrete work orders. Materials flow into the factory from vendors and are consumed based on the work schedule. Hence backflushing is the only logical method that can be used to maintain inventory records.

The two ways of overcoming the tendency of this method to give poor record quality are: (1) periodical inventories, so errors can be purged from the records, or (2) a very controlled factory environment. Nesting containers so the quantity reported is always correct—special identification of items, for example bar coding to avoid item identification errors, and low work-in-process to force scrap, floor losses, or substitutions to become visible—all help this technique achieve acceptable results.

3 Definitions

A variety of terms such as product structures, recipes, formulations, product specifications, and parts lists, are all routinely used to describe bills of materials. These terms are used by different industries to effectively describe the general subject of product definition. The term "bills of materials" will be used throughout this book for this general subject. Other terms have specific meanings and must be clearly defined, which is the objective of this chapter.

Parts list. A parts list for a product is shown in Fig. 1. It is simply a listing of all parts and sub-assemblies needed to produce a given

FIGURE 1

ENGINEERING PARTS LIST FOR
PART NO. 1200, PENCIL ASSEMBLY

PART NO.	DESCRIPTION	QUANTITY
1102	INSERT	1
2151	REWIND MECHANISM	1
2193	LOCK	1
2587	CLIP	1
3440	BODY	1
4430	BUTTON	1
5874	BARREL	1

item, in this case a pencil. In hard goods manufacturing, the parts list often appears on the drawing of the product, so it rarely matches exactly the way the item is produced in the plant. For example, sub-assemblies or intermediates needed by manufacturing for a variety of reasons are often not included. Hence a parts list as defined here describes a listing of parts needed to make a product, without showing the necessary grouping or sequencing of these to produce the item.

The concept of having on one document a pictorial representation of a product, called a "blue print or drawing", and the call-out of specific parts needed to manufacture this product, has been under attack for quite some time. The advantage is that one document contains all the information necessary to produce the product. There are several disadvantages. One is that one document rarely represents how the product is actually made because of the factory's need for grouping parts together into sub-assemblies for efficiency or to provide inventory stocking points. Hence the one document has to be continually revised to suit manufacturing, putting unwanted demands on engineering personnel. groups items for manufacturing's purposes.

Another disadvantage is engineering changes and the need to implement these in an effective manner. Many times the product picture does not change even though the parts may change. An example is changing the hardware needed to assemble an item from nickel plated steel to stainless steel. The picture is not changed at all. And many times revisions are not implemented in the plant for several weeks or even months because of existing inventories of old material or non-availability of the replacement items. Hence two bills of materials are required at this time, one showing the old configuration and the other the new. This is difficult to do when the parts list exists on the drawing.

Probably the largest single disadvantage is duplication of information and the potential for conflicts with two sets of data. Most manufacturers today use computers for material planning, scheduling, costing, pricing and the various other uses described in Chapter 2. Hence it is vital that the computer data be correct. If this information also exists on drawings the opportunity for error and contradiction increases. Many people will then consider the drawing the master document and emphasize its accuracy when in truth it only serves as a picture of the product. All other activities are in fact driven by the information in the computer.

The computer files that define the product have to be the master and all efforts must be directed to making them accurate. Thus the trend is to separate the pictorial view from the parts list or bills of materials. It is a mixed blessing because of the additional paperwork needed in a plant to describe the product; however, the additional flexibility that separation allows often outweighs the disadvantages and opens the door to construct bills of materials more suited to all the uses mentioned earlier.

Family tree. A family tree for the pencil is shown as Fig. 2. Contrary to a parts list, it clearly shows the structural relationship of all purchased and manufactured parts, and how they are grouped together to make the end product. This is a cumbersome way to define a product but one with significant value.

Because of its simple pictorial nature it facilitates seeing the problems in creating one bill of materials to suit all uses. One typical product in every product family should be described using a family tree to assist in the bill of materials evaluation process. Frequently, the key to making bills of materials suit all functional areas is only found after this pictorial display is created and all functions see clearly how to organize the data to suit their needs. Several companies that have done this also found many opportunities for product standardization and cost reduction.

FIGURE 2

FAMILY TREE BoM

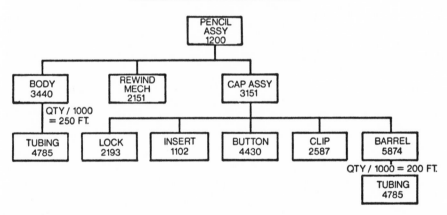

Multi-level or indented. A bill of materials similar to the family tree is the multi-level or, a more normal term used today, indented bill of materials. This is a numerical representation of the product's structure rather than a pictorial display. The numerical level of an item, i.e. how far down in the bill of materials this item exists relative to the finished product, or the indenting of the part number, quantity, or level number, serve to show the structural relationship of the product. In the example for the pencil in Fig. 3, parts 2151, 3440 and 3151, by being indented the same amount, are all components of the parent item, part 1200. Part

FIGURE 3

INDENTED BoM
FOR PENCIL ASSEMBLY

PART NO.	DESCRIPTION	QUANTITY
1200	PENCIL ASSEMBLY	1
2151	REWIND MECHANISM	1
3440	BODY	1
4785	TUBING	0.25 FT.
3151	CAP ASSEMBLY	1
2193	LOCK	1
1102	INSERT	1
4430	BUTTON	1
2587	CLIP	1
5874	BARREL	1
4785	TUBING	0.20 FT.

4785 has two parents, parts 3440 and 5874. Again, this is shown by the indenting of the component under its parent.

This bill of materials condenses the family tree pictorial display but it is not as easy for people unfamiliar with this format to visualize the product make-up as with the family tree approach. However, for the bulk of items this format is useful because of the smaller amount of space needed and the ability to use normal printing devices such as typewriters or computers.

An indented bill of materials has as its primary use the planning of material procurement and the scheduling of the factory. The structure shows the various groupings of parts into higher level items. Combine this with lead times for each process and the location of stocking points, plus some additional inventory information, and the framework for material requirements planning exists.

Single level. A single level bill of materials gets its name from the fact it only contains a parent and its immediate components. This contrasts with the multi-level format which shows all parts and materials at all levels. An example of a single level bill of materials is shown as Fig. 4. This is a piece of the pencil shown in Fig. 2. The cap assembly, part 3151, has five immediate components. Each of these appear on the

FIGURE 4

SINGLE LEVEL BoM
FOR PART NO. 3151, CAP ASSEMBLY

COMPONENT PART NO.	DESCRIPTION	QUANTITY
2193	LOCK	1
1102	INSERT	1
4430	BUTTON	1
2587	CLIP	1
5874	BARREL	1

single level bill of materials but the tubing, part 4785, because it is at a secondary level from the cap assembly, is excluded. It is the sole component on the single level bill of materials for the barrel, part 5874.

This form of bill of materials is the way computers store information describing the structure of products. A series of single level bills of materials are required to define a complete product. For example, the pencil assembly requires four single level bills of materials for parts 1200, 3440, 3151, and 5874 to define it completely.

The reason computers store bills of materials this way is that structural information describing a sub-assembly or component is only stored once. No matter where this sub-assembly or component is used the same bill of materials will be retrieved by the computer. This contrasts with having to store complete multi-level bills of materials for every product and hence having duplication wherever commonality exists. With single level bills of materials in a computer, multi-level print-outs can be made by simply "chaining" together a whole series of the single level relationships.

This single level approach assists in maintenance activities because, regardless of how many times the same sub-assembly or component is used to make parent items, only one set of data needs to be updated with changes or revisions. Hence it improves bill of materials accuracy and also minimizes the amount of stored information, allowing computer files to be smaller.

A print-out of this bill of materials is often used when issuing manufacturing instructions. An assembly foreman is rarely interested in the materials his components are made from. All he needs to know is which components are necessary to make the assembly. Hence a single level bill of materials provides him with just the information he needs. Similarly, a pick list for the ingredients to produce an item comes from a single level bill of materials.

Summarized. A summarized bill of materials groups all like components in a product and totals the quantity of each component used in that product. Structural relationships are not shown. An example for the pencil assembly is shown in Fig. 5. The tubing is used to make two different items but it is only listed once with the total quantity needed to make a finished pencil. It is similar to the engineering parts list except it summarizes all single level bills of materials needed to make an item, including raw materials.

This format is often useful as an accuracy check. Significant errors in quantities and missing items sometimes stand out better with a summarized picture than they do with either single level or indented bills of materials.

FIGURE 5

SUMMARIZED BILL OF MATERIAL
FOR PENCIL ASSY #1200

PART NO.	DESCRIPTION	QUANTITY
1102	INSERT	1
2151	REWIND MECHANISM	1
2193	LOCK	1
2587	CLIP	1
3151	CAP ASSEMBLY	1
3440	BODY	1
4430	BUTTON	1
4785	TUBING	0.45 FT.
5874	BARREL	1

Where-used reports/traceability. A where-used report is the same information as in a bill of materials but resorted from a parent/component to a component/parent relationship. An example is shown in Fig. 6. The two parents of the tubing, part 4785, are listed with the quantity of tubing needed to make one unit of the parent.

FIGURE 6

SINGLE LEVEL WHERE-USED
FOR PART NO. 4785, TUBING

PART NO.	DESCRIPTION	QUANTITY
5874	BARREL	0.20 FT.
3440	BODY	0.25 FT.

This resorted format is useful when implementing engineering changes. When considering a change to an item, all the parents that utilize this item must be evaluated to see if the change can apply in all places or only in some of them. In the latter case, additional part numbers are required to effect the change.

This traceability feature is also useful when materials or parts are scarce or inadequate to service all needs. By identifying the end products that use them, decisions can be made on how best to allocate the available supplies to the right item.

The where-used capability is also used when costing a product. A costing "roll-up" starts from purchased material prices and works its way up the bill of materials adding standard labor and overhead or burden costs from the routings or process standards until reaching the finished product level.

A modified version of the where-used capability is called "pegging," which frequently exists in conjunction with a material requirements planning program. Pegging is described more fully in Chapter 5.

Batch Bills of Materials. Some industries, especially the pharmaceutical or chemical industries, define bills of materials not to make one unit of an end item but to manufacture a batch of end items. This is because some materials used in the process are not used in direct proportion to the quantity of product produced; only a certain amount is required regardless of the batch size. An example is the amount of yeast required to make wine ferment; this is not in direct relationship to the volume of wine in the container.

The best examples of batch bills of materials are the recipes in a cook book. The number of people that can be served by this recipe or the quantity of food produced are almost always given. If half as much is required, simply halving the quantities of ingredients in the recipe will not provide the same texture or taste as the original recipe. There is a synergism among the ingredients that is affected by changing the volumes in the mix. Hence a bill of materials in this environment must always be to manufacture a given batch of product. If varying size batches are produced, then different bills of materials are required, linked to the specific batch quantity.

Phantom or Pseudo bills of materials. These names do not have a clear definition in industry. As used in this book, a phantom bill of materials describes a grouping of items that does not flow in and out of a stocking point. An example is a sub-assembly made on a feeder line but consumed almost immediately by the major assembly line production. The bill of materials is real in that the item exists but it is transparent to the inventory planning system. If pick lists are generated for the finished product, the explosion of the bill of materials will "blow through" this item to its components.

A pseudo bill of materials is a grouping of items that cannot be made and are usually grouped, either to simplify bill of materials maintenance or to assist in master production scheduling. A good example is a kit of hardware, always used to make a variety of finished products, but grouped together to simplify the hardware call-out. The inventory system treats this item the same as a phantom; that is, it "blows through" it when planning or creating pick lists, but the reason for this bill of materials existence is quite different to the phantom. Some of the confusion over the meaning of these two words is because the inventory system treats them the same.

Phantom and pseudo are both very important terms to manufacturing control systems. They provide the facility for some of the multiple uses of bills of materials mentioned in Chapter 2. We will see in later chapters how to use these effectively, especially the pseudo bill of materials.

4   Data Elements

The majority of manufacturers today use computers to assist them with their business information needs. As bills of materials are such key sets of information and computers so adept at retrieving and sorting data in different ways, it is worthwhile understanding some of the elements and organizational relationships that are possible when computers are utilized. This does not mean many of these concepts are invalid without computers, just that they are easier to handle with the data manipulation power of a computer.

Bills of materials are stored in a computer quite differently to their pictorial representation. Here is one place where what you see is not necessarily what you get! A good analogy is a phone book. How does the phone company store data in its computers that links, name, address and phone number? The data could be stored in phone number sequence, yet it is printed alphabetically. It could just as easily be stored randomly as long as an index allows retrieval of the desired information.

Many people confuse the two, storage of data and retrieval of data. When users speak to data processing people, they often say, "The bill of materials must be just like this." What they mean is that the *print-out* must be just like this. How it is stored is of little consequence to the user but of vital importance to data processing. Some of the more important considerations of data relationships and content will be discussed in this chapter, providing clues to how the power of computers can be harnessed to satisfy all uses of bills of materials from one common set of stored information.

Item Master Data

Bills of materials information can be split into two discretely different segments. The first segment is referred to as the item master information and is all data that pertains to an item or part except for its linkage to other items. Item master data elements are part number, description, unit of measure, cost, how many are in inventory, commodity codes, inventory classification, and a whole host of other codes and information. One item master record is required for every part number or raw material called out on a bill of materials.

Product Structure Data

The second data segment is called product structure information which defines the structural relationships of an item. It performs the linking of parent items to their components and components to their parents. One product structure record is needed whenever two parts are linked together. For example, to describe the cap assembly in Fig. 2, five product structure records are necessary, linking the cap assembly to its immediate components. Another product structure is required to link the barrel to the tubing. Seven item master records are needed, one for each part.

Retrieving and sorting these two sets of data in a variety of ways allows a computer to generate different pictorial representations from essentially the same information; for example, single level, indented, and summarized bills of materials and the reverse, where-used reports. What you see in a computer file is not necessarily what you get on a print-out! It depends on the specific programs written to access the information and the way it is presented to suit the user.

Low Level Coding

A huge variety of codes are used both by the computer and the users of information to identify an item's specific characteristics. One of these, mainly of use to a computer, is an item's low level code. This is automatically assigned to all items as product structure linkages are made. It is the numerical value of the lowest level at which the item appears in any bill of materials. For example, in the pencil bill of materials of Fig. 2, part number 4785 has a low level code of 3. The pencil assembly is at level 0 and levels are incremented numerically down the bill of materials. The low level code of 3 is assigned to part number 4785 even though it appears at both levels 2 and 3. It is always the *lowest* level where an item appears in any bill of materials.

There are two basic reasons for assigning low level codes. One is to let computerized material requirements planning programs know when to net the requirements for a part against its on-hand and on-order inventory. Again referencing the pencil's bill of materials of Fig. 2, when the bill of materials is exploded from level 1 to level 2, plans to produce more 3440s will generate requirements for the raw material, 4785. But additional tubing may be required to make some 5874s. It is not until the bill of materials is exploded from level 2 to level 3, 4785's low level code, that all needs are known. The low level code assures that material requirements planning has calculated the total requirements for materials 4785 before they are netted against its on-hand inventory and scheduled procurements.

The second reason for low level codes is costing. Costing programs start at the lowest level in a bill of materials and "roll" costs upwards; the low level code is a convenient way of starting this costing roll-up. When selectively costing one product rather than all products, low level coding does not apply. In this case, it is the lowest level at which parts appear in this product's bill of materials that is important, not the low level code. This is normally determined by a selective explosion of this bill of materials and is sometimes called relative level coding.

Sequencing The Print-out

As mentioned in Chapter 2, it is frequently necessary to list parts on a bill of materials in a predetermined sequence so the bill of materials can also serve as manufacturing instructions. Without the additional coding to perform this sequencing, items usually appear on a bill of materials print-out in part number sequence. The sequence code is made part of the product structure data. When a bill of materials is retrieved, all parts can then be sorted in the desired sequence before printing.

A sequence number also allows the same part number to appear many times on the same single level bill of materials. Without it, a part number can only exist once with the total quantity required. Having the

FIGURE 7

BALLOONING

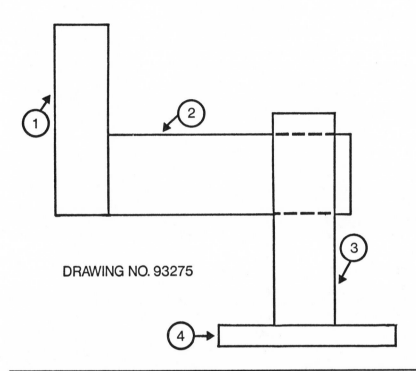

DRAWING NO. 93275

FIND NO.	PART NO.	DESCRIPTION	QTY. REQD.	UNIT OF MEASURE
1	39265	ARM	1	EACH
2	43276	SHAFT	1	EACH
3	24763	BRACKET	1	EACH
4	76329	FOOT	1	EACH

BILL OF MATERIAL
PART NO. 93275

same part listed several times is often necessary on an assembly bill of materials used for manufacturing instructions. For example, a common bolt, used to join a variety of parts at different steps in the assembly process, must be printed several times, always below the items it joins. The sequence number supports this feature.

Another use of the sequence number is as a "find" number when linking bills of materials and drawings. The technique of "ballooning", identifying parts on a drawing with a numeric code, can also be part of the sequence number on a bill of materials as shown in Fig. 7. Ballooning allows separation of the two documents, drawings and bills of materials, and pulls them back together, linking their information.

Departmental Coding

Many times bills of materials need to be different for each department. For example, engineering defines a product one way but manufacturing builds it another way for efficiency or inventory stocking considerations. Sometimes costing needs information no one else uses, especially when developing definitive product line costs. In these cases, bills of materials print-outs must be customized to suit each functional group without each group's specific needs interfering with the other's. This can be done by coding each part to the function, whether it is engineering, cost, or production related, or combinations and permutations of all these. Codes allow a bill of materials to be retrieved and presented to suit each functional group. An example is shown in Fig. 8 where a variety of bills of materials print-outs can be generated from the same basic data, and the data then used for a variety of purposes. For example, the label will only appear on the costing bill of materials and be included only in the costing roll-up. It will be ignored by all other programs, such as material requirements planning. Coding is one of the key techniques that makes it possible for one common set of bill of materials data to do many different jobs.

As soon as the idea of coding items to suit different functional needs is accepted, it will resolve many of the conflicts between what should be included in a bill of materials and what should be omitted. Many times engineers and cost accountants want bills of materials completely defined, including hardware and supply items. However, because purchasing buys these in bulk and they are issued into the factory without regard to their specific usage, material control does not need them on their

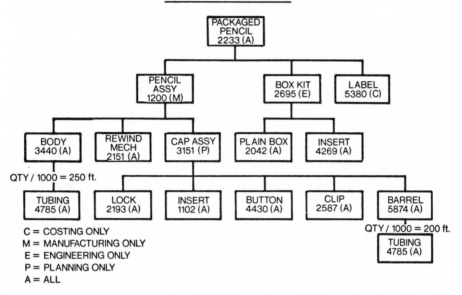

FIGURE 8

BoM CODING

bills of materials. Coding these parts "engineering and costing only" eliminates them from planning and scheduling and now one common set of data suits all groups.

Items Included

A lot of controversy exists over which items should or should not be in a bill of materials.

Many items, especially those sold to consumers, must have packaging in the bill of materials because the product cannot be sold without it. Sometimes the packaging even forms part of the display stand. Most groups agree in this environment that packaging belongs in the bills of materials. However, other products need different packaging, sometimes to suit the specific customer or for domestic versus export sales. In this case, packaging is frequently not in bills of materials and engineers resist adding it. Yet it has to be planned and scheduled, and it is part of the product cost, so a definition of the packaging is required to suit planning and costing. Departmental coding allows those groups who need it to have packaging included for their purposes and omitted from others.

Other items can benefit greatly from being included in bills of materials but rarely are included. An example is a company making bearings where specific grinding wheels are needed to manufacture different bearings. The usual method of ordering consumable tools, such as grinding wheels, is to keep track of average historical usage and use this to plan for the future. However, many bearings are made in batches intermittently throughout the year. An average usage of one grinding wheel per week could be caused by using ten grinding wheels all at once to make a batch of bearings every ten weeks. Having two or three wheels in stock, based on average usage, when a production lot is scheduled is of no value whatsoever.

In this case, grinding wheels should be planned just as any other materials to coincide with bearing production. But to do this means adding grinding wheels to the bill of materials, as in Fig. 9, with the quantity usage an estimate of the life of the wheel, with probably some contin-

FIGURE 9

BILL OF MATERIAL CONTENT

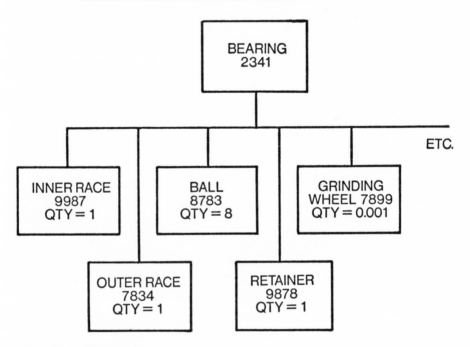

gency to cover the variability of wheel performance. Coding the grinding wheels "planning only" will prevent them appearing on the engineer's bill of materials.

An interesting thought now develops for costing. Consumable tools are frequently unique to a product with highly variable costs for each tool. With each tool linked to a specific product through bills of materials, it is possible not only to plan adequate tools to suit production, but also to have more accurate product costs. This is certainly better than spreading the total consumable tool budget over all products through an overhead rate, the usual way of allocating tool costs to products, even though the tool life is an estimate and can be a somewhat variable figure.

Costing may also need other items in bills of materials nobody else wants. An example is a metal building manufacturer, making products for both North and South areas of America. Buildings in the North need stronger roofs and supporting structures because of the possibility of snow loads; those in the South can get away with a lighter framework. Bills of materials define the specific structures for each type of building so these differences between Northern and Southern varieties can be costed accurately.

However, one expensive supply item used to make these buildings that is not normally included in bills of materials is welding rod, used to join the various steel sections. The amount of welding rod required to produce a Northern building is significantly higher than that required for Southern buildings. Arbitrarily allocating welding rod purchases through an overhead rate or pro-rating it to the costs of finished products does not distribute these costs correctly. Cost estimates for Northern buildings are under-stated and for Southern buildings over-stated. But by adding estimates of the amount of welding rod needed for Northern and Southern buildings in their bills of materials, costing can be more accurate. These items will probably be coded "costing only" as engineering has no interest in knowing how much welding rod is required and production will buy rod on an average usage basis.

This same logic can be applied to many other items, traditionally thought of as supply items. Grease, paint, glue and cleaning solvents are all examples of items many companies now list on their bills of materials because of the value the extra data provides.

Another area of contention, especially in hard goods manufacturing, is whether raw materials should be defined by the design engineers when they write the bills of materials. Many design engineers feel they should only specify purchased and manufactured items; materials, such as sheet, bar, tube or coil, should only be referenced with the material specification number. Their logic is that the specific way of making these parts has to be defined first, usually a manufacturing engineer's function, before the material call-out can be completed. Bar or tube could be used to make a tubular item, sheet or coil to make a sheet metal item, and the decision should be based on buying materials and making the part for the lowest cost. Design engineers do not make this decision, so leave this information off their bills of materials.

However, the information is needed for costing, material procurement and picking the right materials from stores. It is also useful to have when engineers change designs so the full ramifications on material procurement, standard materials, and revisions to costs can be considered before making the change. Now it means getting bills of materials completed by the design engineers after the manufacturing process is defined or having a separate group, such as manufacturing engineering, complete them. This idea of sole or split responsibility for bills of materials maintenance will be discussed further in Chapter 8, Accuracy.

A similar problem exists between identifying machined and rough castings. Many design engineers consider these two items the same and assign one part number to describe both. But inventories could be maintained of both rough and machined castings and it is important to know how many of each are in stock to plan additional casting procurement, the capacity needed to machine them, and the cost involved. Hence, two part numbers are needed to identify the rough and machined castings with a product structure linking the two parts together.

As a general statement, a bill of materials is not complete until all legs of the product structure chains end in either a purchased part or purchased raw material. Referencing Fig. 2 again, parts 4785, 2151, 2193, 1102, 4430 and 2587 must all be purchased. If any of them are manufactured in this plant, the bill of materials is not complete and will not be until the legs end in a purchased item.

There are a few exceptions to this worth noting. A company manufacturing a product from castings they produce in their own foundry will rarely take the time to define the casting's raw materials. Pig iron, scrap, chemicals, sand, and parting compounds are usually planned on a bulk basis. Hence, this chain could validly end in a manufactured part. Other exceptions are customer furnished materials and reference items. See Chapter 8 for a further discussion of the contents of bills of materials and how to ensure they are complete.

Another area of conflict is the manufacturing of a part both inside and outside the plant. Some parts have operations performed on them internally, go outside for further processing, for example heat treating or plating, and return either as completed parts or go back into the plant for completion. As far as the designers are concerned, they want a finished part produced to their specification and how it is done is of little or no interest to them. Hence, they assign a part number to the finished part and a part number to the starting raw material or purchased part needed to make it, with a product structure linking the two. The designer has done his job.

But along comes inventory control, concerned about keeping track of what parts are at what stage of manufacture for future planning. And accounting is interested in knowing how much of the company's assets are at the vendor's facility, their recovery of all of them, and correctly paying for the work performed. A part number is the universal common language in a plant to perform these tasks but the designer only assigned a part number to the finished part. This is obviously inadequate to provide the inventory planning and fiscal control needed by other functions.

There are two different approaches to solve this problem. One is to assign a part number defining the part as it leaves the plant, another when it returns, and another if it gets further finishing operations before completion. All these parts are chained together using product structure linkages; the intermediate parts are coded manufacturing and costing only, eliminating them from the design engineers documentation.

Another way of solving this control problem is to use the routing or process sheet as the identifier of parts at intermediate stages of manufacture. This takes a routing as well as a bill of materials, linked together, with both in-plant and outside operations defined. The part number is then modified by the operational step, in essence a different part number to the system, and control occurs to this modified identifier.

Which of these two to use depends on a number of factors. First, is there a well defined routing system in place, linked to the parts being produced with operational steps included for outside processing? Second, are the inventory, accounting and purchasing control systems designed to accept part numbers modified or identified to the operational step of manufacture? If these two can be answered yes, then the second way of solving the control problems is best because it allows more flexibility in manufacturing products without involving design engineers in things that do not concern them. If either question is answered no, then the first way will be necessary with provisions now made for design engineers or some other function to add the necessary new parts, product structure linkages, and departmental codes.

The value of coding items to suit a department's needs can be extended to many items. All functions have their specific needs that are of no interest to the others, so coding the parts to the function allows specific bills of materials to be generated to suit each particular need. The deciding factors on what to include or leave out of bills of materials must be the costs to maintain the data and the value derived from it. If the payback is good, include it; if not leave it out.

Delivery Point Codes

In a large assembly plant, when items are picked from a stockroom to support a given production run or specific manufactured item, the parts have to be delivered to a defined location close to where they will be assembled. An example is a plant assembling gasoline pumps where the length of the manufacturing lines is several hundred feet. The base of the pump must be delivered to the start of the line but the internal components need to be delivered to various stages along the line. The sheet metal doors, the last things to go on the pump before it is put into a carton, are needed at the end of the line.

Many times the same item is used on a variety of products made on separate lines. Hence, when the total quantity of parts for a given pro-

FIGURE 10

DELIVERY POINT CODING

PRODUCT STRUCTURES

PARENT PART NO.	COMPONENT PART NO.	QTY / PARENT	DELIVERY POINT
8359	2763	2	106
3976	2842	4	235
4769	2842	1	392
5829	2763	1	441

PICK LIST

PART NO.	QUANTITY TO PICK	DELIVER TO	QUANTITY TO DELIVER
2763	34	106	10
		441	24
2842	25	235	16
		392	9

duction run are withdrawn from stock, the amount of material picked must be split up between the various lines needing some of this common item. This can be done through delivery point codes added in the product structure linkages as shown in Figure 10. When the picking information is created, it shows the total number of parts required but also allocates the quantities to be sent to each specific location. This assists material handlers in delivering parts correctly.

A slight modification to this is necessary when products frequently change assembly lines. Again, referring back to gasoline pumps, a variety of pumps are manufactured, such as the Mobil round pump, Chevron square pump, or a more standard design purchased by other oil companies. Depending on the volume of sales to each company, one or more lines are assigned to these products. If delivery point codes are built into the product structure linkages, every time a product changes from one line to another, a massive maintenance of the linkages to change the delivery point codes is necessary. To avoid this, the product structure linkages can be simply coded with each item's relative position on the line where it is assembled. For instance, the base is required at location 1 which is always the early part of the line. The sheet metal doors, the last things to be assembled, always go on at position 9, the end of the line. All other items are coded depending on their assembly position. A simple

FIGURE 11

DELIVERY POINT CROSS-REFERENCE

PRODUCT STRUCTURES

PARENT PART NO.	MODEL TYPE	COMPONENT PART NO.	QTY / PARENT	DELIVERY CODE
7394	MOBIL	3986	2	9
6357	CHEVRON	8746	1	4
8629	EXXON	4322	4	5

CROSS REFERENCE

MODEL TYPE \ DELIVERY CODE	1	2	3	4	5	6	7	8	9
MOBIL	101	102	394	104	286	106	107	432	109
CHEVRON	201	386	203	204	286	206	207	382	209
EXXON	301	302	394	304	286	306	307	432	309

cross reference, as shown in Fig. 11, now takes each product and decodes these stages to a specific delivery point location. If products are changed between lines, the only maintenance activity is to the cross reference matrix, a very simple task, and the computer stays in step, always giving the correct location for parts delivery.

Routing Linkage

A routing is a description of the steps needed to make an item, showing the specific machine or work center where these steps will be performed and providing an estimate of the standard time required to perform each step. An example of a routing is shown in Fig. 12. Some companies link each step of the routing to the specific items in the bills of materials that are added at that manufacturing step, as shown in Fig. 13. In this case, the product structure linkages are coded with the operational sequence number of the routing. With this operation number in the bills of materials, the delivery point codes mentioned earlier can be omitted and the combination of bills of materials and routings provides location information for material delivery.

This linking of the bills of materials to the routing provides other facilities. First, it allows "backflushing", described in Chapter 2, to occur to

FIGURE 12

ROUTING

PART NO. 93275

OPERATION NUMBER	WORK CENTER NUMBER	OPERATION DESCRIPTION	STANDARD HRS/UNIT
10	284	ASSEMBLE ITEMS 1 & 2	0.5
20	392	ASSEMBLE ITEMS 3 & 4	0.3
30	641	COMBINE SUB-ASSEMBLIES 1&2 and 3&4	1.0
40	149	TEST	0.1

FIGURE 13

BILL OF MATERIAL WITH ROUTING LINKAGE

PART NO. 93275

FIND NO.	COMPONENT PART NO.	DESCRIPTION	QTY / PARENT	UNIT OF MEASURE	ROUTING STEP
1	39265	ARM	1	EACH	10
2	43276	SHAFT	1	EACH	10
3	24763	BRACKET	1	EACH	20
4	76329	FOOT	1	EACH	20

each operational step rather than at the end of the manufacturing process for an item. Operational backflushing allows more timely relief of inventory if it has to be used.

Second, the product can be costed at each operational step simply by totaling the labor and material costs defined for that operation. Very detailed costing analyses are now possible with any product coded in this manner.

Third, with a record of what items are in the plant at each stage of manufacture, the work-in-process inventory can be valued very accurately.

This way of obtaining accurate costs and inventory valuations is preferred over another approach sometimes used, which is to assign unique part numbers to each operational step in producing a part as shown in Fig. 14. This technique eliminates the need for separate routing information because all inventory and cost data is built directly into the item masters and product structures. However, the bill of materials contains many levels, depending on the number of operational steps included. So large amounts of computer time are spent, retrieving and then ignoring most items, when running programs for production or engineering. It is a poor way to define a product because it only helps one function, costing, and is of no value, and may even be detrimental, to all other functional groups.

Bills of Labor

Some industries, such as pharmaceuticals and chemicals, create not only bills of materials but also bills of labor using item master and pro-

FIGURE 14

ROUTING BUILT INTO BoM

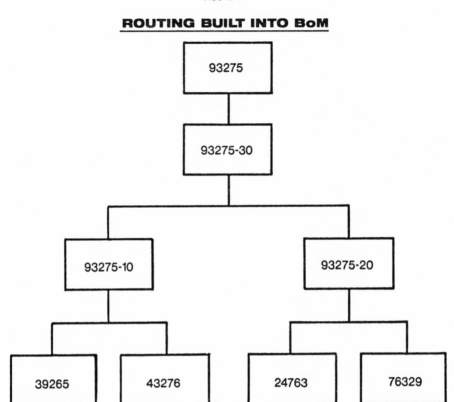

duct structure data. This is quite different to using routings as described above. It results in their being able to get capacity and material information simultaneously. Fig. 15 shows a bill of materials and labor. Part numbers and work centers are both considered item master data. Not only are the quantities of materials needed for an item in the product structure data, but also the number of hours of production resources to make the item. These labor records are normally coded "production only" as it is rare the engineers or accountants are interested in this information. However, when planning to produce quantities of products in the future, the materials needed to manufacture them as well as the hours required are calculated at the same time, especially when using material requirements planning.

A more precise way of planning capacity is separate work center and routing information with scheduling logic to predict when work will arrive in a given work center. This is because the capacity data in bills of

FIGURE 15

BILLS OF MATERIALS AND LABOR

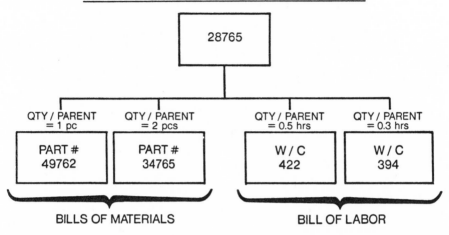

labor is normally summarized to finished products or major assemblies and is rarely time phased correctly. However, for long range, average capacity planning, this is an easy way to get vital information quickly. Some hard goods manufacturers have taken this approach with fast payback for their efforts. It is an opportunity that should not be missed.

Alternate Materials

Many times engineers define a number of equivalent items that can be used to produce a product. Most times these items are completely interchangeable but in a few cases they are not and other material changes have to be made when using certain items.

It is very difficult to define the logic to plan materials when alternates are given. In most cases, one prime item is planned and manual intervention decides which alternate to use when the prime is not available. For example, a low cost resistor with a wide tolerance is adequate for a particular electronic circuit. Obviously, a high cost, closer tolerance resistor with the same nominal resistance value will do the same job. Hence, there is a prime item, the wide tolerance resistor, plus an alternate one with close tolerances. In most cases, all planning will be for the prime item and this is the unit that will be printed on production bills of materials. The alternate is often included in the product structure data but the quantity is usually equal to zero or the item is specially coded to show clearly it is an alternate. No planning will occur for the alternate item and costing programs will ignore it. Manual intervention occurs when supplies of the prime item are inadequate; selection of the alternate is made from its reference on the bill of materials. Sometimes it is known that an alternate item will be used for a while because of extended non-availability of the prime item, or because of large stocks of the alternate that must be used up. This can be controlled through effectivity management, covered in Chapter 7.

Sometimes the design engineer considers items produced by a variety of companies as equals, and there is a need to procure a balanced quantity of items from the various sources. This may be because one source cannot produce enough to satisfy the total demands or simply because of a policy of having multiple sources for an item whenever possible. An example is fractional horsepower motors made by General Electric, Westinghouse, and Reliance Electric. It may be necessary to have a unique part number for each motor because specific customers insist the products they get contain a motor made by a certain vendor or because the motors are not completely interchangeable in all applications.

There are two approaches to this situation. The first is to identify one vendor's product as the prime and the others as alternates. When requisitions are generated to procure motors, purchasing simply splits the total quantity for prime motors between the three vendors based on some pre-established ratio. After the motors are received, they are all stocked under the prime number unless they are not interchangeable.

The second approach is to code all three motors as prime in the bill of materials. The quantity is made a ratio, depending on the desired volume of business to be assigned to each motor manufacturer. Hence, requirements for motors are split automatically between the three vendors. The motors can be carried in stock under their own unique numbers or under one of the numbers as the prime.

Both approaches, although seemingly very logical and straightforward, give severe problems to material control and sometimes cost accounting. If the prime number and alternates method is chosen and the parts are not interchangeable, which means they must be stocked under their own unique numbers, how do you total the three inventories to prevent over buying? And if the ratio method is chosen and one motor has significantly lower inventories than the other two, again, how do you prevent buying more of the one with low inventory when there are plenty of the other two already on-hand?

What does the picking information specify? If the method is prime and alternates, the pick list will always request the prime, failing to rotate stock and use the motors in the desired ratio. Manual intervention will be necessary to select a balanced mix of motors and correctly transmit these decisions to the inventory system.

How do you pick a ratio of a part? If the items have different prices how does cost accounting know which motors were actually used to make which finished products and what price do they use to calculate costs for the finished product? In most cases an arbitrary decision will have to be made and any errors cleaned out when the inventory is valued at year's end.

Things can get very sticky when a customer requests a specific vendor's item for his product, for example a motor made by a certain vendor. Most procurement activities occur well ahead of the receipt of a customer's order, so when his order arrives, special handling is required to determine whether the right motors are in stock and available for that customer. This is best handled by exception on a manual basis. The actual inventories on-hand must be checked to see how many of that vendor's motors are in stock and a reservation placed against them for that specific customer. If the supplies on-hand are inadequate, a special requisition must be sent to purchasing for quick procurement action.

It is very difficult to keep the costing and inventory valuation programs straight with alternates in bills of materials, especially if they have different costs. Margin analysis and inventory valuations can be subject to large errors. This is best controlled through establishment of a secondary set of information for all shop orders open in a plant. Each order is defined originally by its standard bill of materials and routing, but as alternates are chosen, the shop order information is updated to show which materials and operations will be used. In this way the treatment of inventories and recording of costs can be handled correctly.

This secondary file defining orders running in the plant can be used when modifying bills of materials and routings for a variety of reasons. Additional operations required because a batch of material is below standard can be included. The alternates mentioned earlier and sometimes effectivity of change are best handled through a secondary order file showing the current production configuration with the primary bill of materials and routing files showing the latest version. It is a good way to segregate more of the needs of cost accounting and production from the requirements of the engineers.

Alternates in bills of materials are a great idea if not taken too far, but they do present real problems to the precision mathematics of material planning systems, cost accounting and inventory valuation. Make sure the benefits really outweigh the costs before using them and then consider whether manual intervention, which will be required in almost all cases to control them correctly, is not better than using a complex computer system.

Interplant Coding

Many manufacturers have multiple plants, either to serve regional markets or simply because of production volume. Sometimes these plants are completely autonomous, being responsible for their own procurement and manufacture of all items they need, and sometimes they exist as feeder and user plants. In both cases, assuming there is at least some centralized data processing, there is a need to know what inventories are in what plant and in what stage.

In the simplest form, where products are all made the same way in each plant, interplant coding can be handled by the inventory recording system which treats the various plants as stocking locations. This gives some problems to the planning system, as the logic of which inventories are available to satisfy requirements from any one plant must be defined. But this is not too difficult to do in most cases.

The tougher job is when various plants make the same products in different ways or using different materials. This can be solved by using plant codes as part of the product identification or assigning completely different part numbers to the products depending on where they are made. In both cases, additional logic is needed in the planning and cost accounting programs to recognize the finished items are the same even though they were made differently and are either defined with plant codes or different part numbers.

These problems are minimized with distributed data processing and small computers in each plant. Each plant can have its own data on its own computer and the only transition problem is when all the plants link their data together for overall planning or consolidation of financial reports.

5

The Manufacturing Control System

As discussed in Chapter 1, the most significant pressure for change within bills of materials has come from developments in the application of formal systems to the control of a manufacturing business. The need for a coordinated and integrated system that all functions contribute to, gain from, and work in harmony with has provided the impetus to change old ways of information flow and presentation. The two specific techniques within manufacturing control systems that relate to bills of materials are called material requirements planning and master production scheduling. Both will be described in enough detail for the reader to see the connection to bills of materials and the demands these two techniques place on their structure.

Material Requirements Planning

The technique of material requirements planning was developed when the first item was manufactured. A cave man making spears used a mental image of a bill of materials calling for a straight piece of wood, a sharp piece of stone and something to attach them together. The decision of how many spears to make was exploded through the bill of materials to calculate how many of each component he needed. In its simplest form, this explosion was material requirements planning, although an informal variety.

A dinner party is planned using material requirements planning. The number of guests and menu dictates the size and variety of the meal. The recipe (bill of materials) is exploded and the total ingredients calculated. Inventory in cupboards, the refrigerator and freezer is compared to the requirements and shortages identified. A shopping list is the result.

A house is built using material requirements planning. The completion date for the house dictates when the foundation must be poured, when the walls and roof must be erected, when plumbing, electrical work and heating must be in place and when the inside must be finished. These schedules for each activity also dictate when specific materials must be on site, calculated from the house bill of materials.

Hence, material requirements planning has two functions. It can schedule related activities and it can calculate how much material is required. By considering available inventories it can also define potential shortages.

When this technique is transferred to a factory, some additional considerations emerge. First, a factory has not only inventories of finished components and materials in the plant, but also outstanding orders to procure or produce more. The schedules for all these orders must support the planned manufacture of product. Second, products are often manufactured repetitively, if not on a continuous flow basis at least intermittently. Hence, several production runs may be scheduled for different future dates. Third, many items are common to a variety of end products so the total amount of these items needed to support all the end products must be calculated.

An example of material requirements planning in a factory making pens and pencils with commonality of parts is shown in Fig. 16. The pen and pencil production schedules, i.e. the start dates and quantities of assembly, are set and the requirements for all first level items calculated using the bills of materials. This is only shown for the cap assembly, a common part, but the logic is the same for all first level items. These requirements are netted first against the inventory on-hand and then against open factory orders. A negative inventory condition indicates a need to obtain more cap assemblies. The normal lot size is 20 units. These have a lead time to produce; hence, the need date is backed off by the lead time to arrive at a start date for each planning production lot. The start of cap assembly manufacture is the date its components are required. The quantity needed comes from the explosion of the bill of materials and is shown for the lock only. The same logic applies to all second level items. Again, netting of requirements against on-hand inventory and open orders discloses shortages, showing a need to obtain more components. This logic is repeated down through the bill of materials one level at a time so the total demands on any one item can be predicted, its inventories checked against the demands and any necessary replenishment orders planned. The role of low level coding, described in Chapter 4, may now be clearer. Its function is to control when the netting routine can occur because it determines when the total requirements for a part have been calculated.

It is sometimes necessary to identify where requirements for a particular item come from. This may be because it is in short supply or because of capacity constraints affecting its scheduling. Pegging is the term used to keep track of the part that causes a lower level item to have a requirement. It is a form of where-used report created during the material requirements planning calculation and is shown in Fig. 17 for both the lock and cap assembly. It can define not only the parent items that use a part but also how many are needed and when. This is especially useful when requirements for an item, common to a variety of parents, bunch up together in the same period. Pegging keeps track of how many requirements come from each parent.

FIGURE 16

MATERIALS REQUIREMENTS PLANNING

BILL OF MATERIALS

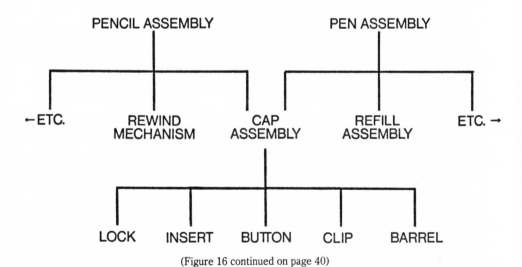

(Figure 16 continued on page 40)

(Figure 16 continued)

PRODUCTION SCHEDULES

WEEK NO.	1	2	3	4	5	6	7	8	9	10
PENCIL	10			10			10			10
PEN		6			6			6		

CAP ASSEMBLY PLANNING

ON HAND = 12   LEAD TIME = 2   SAFETY STOCK = 1

LOT SIZE = 20   PUR / MFG = MFG

WEEK NO.	PAST DUE	1	2	3	4	5	6	7	8	9	10
REQUIREMENTS		10	6	0	10	6	0	10	6	0	10
AVAILABLE INV	11	1	15	15	5	−1	−1	−11	−17	−17	−27
OPEN SHOP ORDERS			20								
PLANNED RECEIPTS						20					20
PLANNED RELEASES				20					20		

LOCK PLANNING

ON HAND = 4   LEAD TIME = 4   SAFETY STOCK = 0

LOT SIZE = LOT FOR LOT   PUR/MFG = PUR

WEEK NO.	PAST DUE	1	2	3	4	5	6	7	8	9	10
REQUIREMENTS				20					20		
AVAILABLE INV	4	4	4	2	2	2	2	2	−18	−18	−18
OPEN PURCHASE ORDERS				18							
PLANNED RECEIPTS									18		
PLANNED RELEASES					18						

Many people, seeing the simplicity and straightforward logic of material requirements planning, question what other way there might be to plan inventories and schedule a plant. It *was* used almost exclusively in the early days of manufacturing, but products became more complex, and the marketplace pressures demanded faster changes. It was just not possible manually to perform all the necessary calculations and revise them frequently enough. So material requirements planning was discarded in favor of statistical models for part and material usage, resulting in the order point technique, applied to one item at a time without the huge number of calculations material requirements planning demands. The order point technique functions well in some areas such as warehouse replenishment but poorly in manufacturing planning. Extra cushions of inventory and the informal technique of expediting kept most plants operating during the early days of manufacturing. But then along came computers and the restraint of not being able to make a large number of calculations quickly disappeared; material requirements planning was reborn. And not just back to the original manual version, but with

FIGURE 17

PEGGING

LOCK

WEEK NO.	QUANTITY	PARENT
3	20	CAP ASSEMBLY
8	20	CAP ASSEMBLY

CAP ASSEMBLY

WEEK NO.	QUANTITY	PARENT
1	10	PENCIL
2	6	PEN
4	10	PENCIL
5	6	PEN
7	10	PENCIL
8	6	PEN
10	10	PENCIL

enhancements that have thrust it into its current status of being the backbone of most manufacturing control systems in existence today.

Future developments will change the simplistic scheduling logic of material requirements planning but will not remove the need for a structural linkage of parents and components, the bill of materials. If anything, additional demands will be placed on this critical set of data to support advances in planning and scheduling as we move towards automated hard goods factories.

Master Production Scheduling

A master production schedule is a formal plan defining what products will be made in a plant, how many, and when, as a minimum covering the composite horizon of lead times necessary to procure materials and process them through the plant. This minimum horizon is shown in Fig. 18 and is simply the stacking up of the critical path lead times to pur-

FIGURE 18

MASTER PRODUCTION SCHEDULE

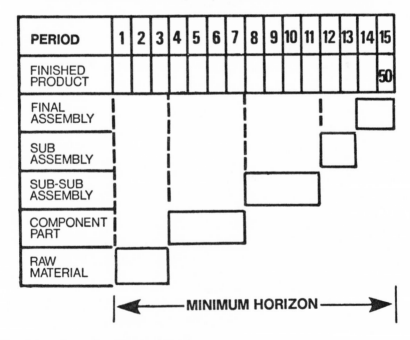

chase materials and manufacture a product assuming no inventory is in the plant. The master production schedule must extend beyond this horizon if additional future visibility is needed.

This numerical representation of the future is exploded through bills of materials using the technique of material requirements planning to give specific information on what materials and parts to buy and what schedules to issue in a plant.

The master production schedule is analogous to the steering wheel of a car. Wherever it is turned the car will go. Whatever numbers are in the master production schedule, material requirements planning will explode, creating demands for all purchased and manufactured items. All functions will now aggressively try to support these demands and execute the master production schedule.

But just as a steering wheel of a car can be turned in the wrong direction, causing disaster, so can the numbers in the master production schedule be wrong, causing equally disastrous results. Getting the right numbers is one of the severest challenges facing manufacturers today and will be the subject of this section.

A master production schedule can contain booked customer orders, forecasts of customer orders or a combination of the two. Examples of products with booked orders only are ships and custom machinery. In the total world of manufacturing, a company with the full horizon of the master production schedule defined with customer orders is rare.

Examples of products with no booked orders but only forecasts of sales are consumer products: food, some industrial products such as electrical fittings or plumbing supplies, spare parts for cars and trucks, and some pharmaceuticals. Products with combinations of booked orders and forecasts of sales are machine tools, prefabricated metal buildings, telephone exchanges, and large electrical motors.

In all cases, it is the numbers in the master production schedule exploded through bills of materials, that provide the information of what items to buy and make to support customer's orders or anticipated desires. Hence the making of a valid master production schedule controls inventory levels and customer service simultaneously. Many plants provide poor service to customers at the same time that they have high inventories because of their inability to provide this kind of master production schedule. Much of this problem can be traced directly to a failure to structure the bills of materials correctly.

In Fig. 18, purchasing is ordering materials today for numbers in the master production schedule at the end of the critical path of the stacked lead times, i.e. for period 15. Many companies glibly talk about lead times of six months, nine months, or even eighteen months to produce their product from the time of placing a purchase order for materials until they have a product ready to ship to a customer. If the bulk of this horizon is based on forecasts, and most master production schedules are, then it is the ability to predict the future sales of products that controls the quality of the numbers in the master production schedule. And it is this ability that will trigger purchasing to buy and manufacturing to make either the right or wrong materials in the right or wrong amounts for the right or wrong delivery dates. And on these decisions rests the profitability and success of a manufacturing concern.

Some people believe they can shorten this critical path time by carrying stocks of materials or parts. But on what basis are these stocks provided? If they are based on past history they will control that the future master production schedule must be approximately equal to the past, hence the inventory decisions have caused an informal master production schedule to exist over the critical path horizon.

Forecasts

Four basic characteristics of forecasts must be understood when developing a master production schedule. Each characteristic will be studied in turn and some thoughts developed to include in the manufacturing planning process.

a. Forecasts are almost always wrong. Just look at predictions for the stock market, the country's economy or the weather to confirm this statement. As fast as forecasts are made they are revised and changed as new information becomes available and as actual behaviour is different to what was expected. But forecasts of the future are all we have in many cases, and are certainly a base to plan from. So effort and attention is needed to make the best forecast possible, which in many cases will mean defining the product differently, and in some cases even designing the product differently.

b. Forecasts should be two numbers or preferably three. If forecasts are almost always wrong, then the question is how wrong. In most cases, the error in forecasts is more predictable than the forecast itself. If it is difficult or impossible to forecast an event accurately, such as how many of a given product customers will buy in a given time period, then a range which encompasses the actual event is a better way of predicting the future. For example, a sales forecast of 340 units, plus or minus 20, the expected error, is a much better forecast than just 340 units. This is actually three forecasts: expected, an upper limit and a lower limit. The reaction of many people is "How will this help me? How are three wrong numbers better than just one wrong number? And how do I put three sets of numbers into my manufacturing control system that was designed for just one, the master production schedule?"

This depends on how the three numbers are used. If they are used effectively to provide contingency planning in the plant, then as customers' orders arrive different from what was forecast, shipments can be made without major plant disruptions or poor customer service being generated. We will see a little later whether this increases inventories in total or whether reductions in total inventory occur because of this contingency planning. The important thing is to recognize a need to segregate the volatile items in a product's bill of materials, that is, those variables difficult to forecast well, from the stable items. Different contingencies can be placed on these two types of items and here we are, back again discussing the make-up of bills of materials.

c. Forecasts are more accurate for families. The larger the statistical population the more predictable the results. The smaller and more specific the data, the more unpredictable the results. This suggests that master production schedules should be constructed for product families or groups wherever possible with conversion of these into specific items delayed until the last possible moment. However, this is not the way most master production schedules are made today. Most of them are expressed in specific product terms because that is the way bills of materials are defined. Different bills of materials, defining product families, are necessary for this characteristic to be built into master production schedules, allowing better procurement of materials and scheduling of factories more in concert with actual demands.

d. Forecasts are more wrong the further out they are made. This is a statistical fact. Predicting an event short range is more accurate than predicting an event a long time in the future. So the longer the minimum horizon of the master production schedule the more times materials and parts will be obtained incorrectly today to suit the actual customer's orders that are booked in the future. This suggests a war on lead times, decreasing them wherever possible to improve the forecast accuracy of the master production schedule. It also suggests that the structure of bills of materials should consider the build-up of lead times and be arranged wherever possible to decrease the critical path for all products.

Zoning the Master Production Schedule

These four forecast characteristics suggest a framework for the master production schedule to combat the problems outlined above. Instead of a master production schedule being viewed as a continuum of information all at the same level of detail, it should be considered a series of time zones where the detail varies to suit the quality of the forecast, as shown in Fig. 19.

Zone 1 is the close-in time frame. The master production schedule is defined using actual booked customer's orders or short range forecasts to replenish warehouses. As this information usually relates to specific end products, a traditional bill of materials can be used in this zone to provide detailed information on which short range activities need to be performed.

In Zone 2, the intermediate time zone, a lower level of detail exists. No customer's orders are booked or perhaps just a few, certainly not

FIGURE 19

MASTER PRODUCTION SCHEDULING TIME ZONES

	ZONE 1	ZONE 2	ZONE 3
MASTER PRODUCTION SCHEDULE DEFINITION	FINISHED PRODUCTS	PRODUCT FAMILIES	PLANT TOTALS
SYSTEM DATA REQUIRED	FINISHED PRODUCT (TRADITIONAL) BoMS DETAILED ROUTINGS	FAMILY BoMS BILLS OF LABOR	AVERAGE MATERIAL AND LABOR CONSUMPTION RATIOS
INFORMATION GENERATED	DETAILED FACTORY SCHEDULES	LONG LEAD TIME ITEM PROCUREMENT	RAW MATERIAL & FEEDSTOCK SCHEDULES
	SHORT LEAD TIME ITEM PROCUREMENT	GROSS FACTORY OPERATING RATES	PLANT & MACHINERY NEEDS

enough to fill the plant capacity. If the product is made to stock, little warehouse replenishment information is available. So the master production schedule must be fleshed out with longer range forecasts. To compensate for the loss of accuracy, a switch to product families must be made both for forecasts and the master production schedule. But now the traditional bill of materials used in Zone 1 is no longer valid. Bills of materials must be available that define *families* of products to provide more accurate procurement and scheduling information for long lead time materials and parts.

In Zone 3, the far out time zone, this thinking process is extended to broad groups of products or even to the total product line. But now a relationship between these broad groups and the raw materials they use has to be established, suggesting yet another bill of materials definition.

Contingency Planning

No matter how much work goes into making better forecasts, the first characteristic says they will still be wrong. There are three fundamental choices at this point. The first is to change the factory and vendor schedules quickly to react to specific customer orders as they are received, different to what was forecast. The penalty is higher factory costs, vendor discontent and high inventories. The second choice is to make what was forecast and promise customer deliveries to fit the master production schedule. The penalty could be customer discontent, lost sales, and high inventories of items made but not yet sold. The third is to add contingency in the master production schedule to allow actual sales to differ from what was planned without significant disturbance to the factory or vendor schedules.

This last approach is the best for the bulk of companies, as it gives stable factory and vendor schedules at the same time as it provides flexibility in the marketplace. If this is done by selectively increasing the master production schedule, it is called "over-planning". In its simplest form, this is simply a rolling bubble of extra numbers in the master production schedule which get exploded through bills of materials and create additional requirements for components and materials over and above the expected demand.

The additional inventory to cover forecast errors is only needed on those parts in the bills of materials with poor predictability of the future. Items common to a whole family of products will have relatively accurate forecasts, and so can be planned by a family master production schedule with little or no contingency. However, items unique to specific finished goods are more difficult to predict with any degree of accuracy. So here is where more contingency or over-planning is needed. But most bills of materials are not organized to allow selective over-planning to occur on just the unique items. They usually define complete finished products so contain both common and unique parts. With these bills of materials it is only possible to add contingency on the unique parts separate from the common ones by planning safety stocks on the unique items. The problem with safety stock applied in this manner is the quantities applied rarely result in matched sets of parts. Hence excess inventory is carried with no compensating improvement in customer service. When a master production schedule item is over-planned, all components in its bill of materials will get a matched amount of safety stock. This results in being able to produce extra finished products if necessary from this planned extra inventory.

And now the question—"Does over-planning result in more or less total inventories?" Without it, the choices are to jerk factory and vendor schedules quickly or to promise customers deliveries that suit a fixed master production schedule. In both cases, total inventories will be high because shipments will not be made consistently. And it is when shipments stop or are delayed that inventories increase the most.

Over-planning, assuming it is sufficient to cover the expected sales variations, will help to keep shipments on time. The small amount of extra inventory caused by these numbers, again depending on the amount of common versus unique parts in a design, will in most cases be more than offset by the reduced inventories of timely shipping. Some companies have seen and vouch for significantly reduced inventories, greatly improved customer service, and reductions in factory disruption, all because of selective over-planning and a well run manufacturing control system.

Another reason for using the master production schedule to plan contingency is that it is highly visible to all management functions. Sales people can relate to the amount of flexibility they are being provided, which is difficult or impossible for them to do when safety stocks are applied to individual components in a complex bill of materials. Accountants can cost out the amount of excess inventory and question the return on investment. Manufacturing can estimate the amount of flexibility they must be prepared to handle and the costs and impact of making these changes. And engineering can question their designs to see how to simplify and standardize the products with the objective of reducing inventories and improving customer service.

Master production schedules need different bills of materials than the traditional ones. They must define product families, and separate unique groupings from the common parts whenever possible. They must be constructed to improve the quality of forecasts and to allow contingency planning through the master production schedule. These are the objectives that will be used when discussing various types of bills of materials in Chapter 6.

6 Types of Bills of Materials

In Chapter 3, various presentation formats for bills of materials were described. Chapter 4 advanced the concept of including many different items such as tooling and labor information. Also in Chapter 4 was a discussion of coding items in bills of materials depending on their specific end use.

The structuring concepts from this chapter will be combined with the coding concepts of Chapter 4 to show how one common set of data can be used to create output information to suit a wide variety of end uses. The key concept is that a bill of materials simply links one part to another and this linkage can be created in any way that suits the uses described in Chapter 2. It is the skill of organizing the data, its coding, and the retrieval programs, that allow one system to support all users.

As described in Chapter 5, there are three primary objectives for structuring a bill of materials differently to the way an engineer traditionally defines the product:

1. to forecast as accurately as possible.
2. to apply contingency to those items that have a low quality forecast.
3. to consider the need for zoning of the master production schedule.

These three objectives will be the framework of this chapter.

Modular Bills

Many companies make finished products from a variety of options customers select. The classical example is automobiles, where customers select such items as body style, engine size, transmission type, seat configuration, upholstery fabrics and colors, radios, air conditioning, and many, many more. Another good example is machine tools, where a basic machine usually has a wide variety of options available for it to perform a number of different functions. The packaging of bulk products, such as aspirin, into a variety of different containers can be considered as producing to customer option, the customer in this case being a warehouse or distribution center. In many companies with these types of products, bills of materials are defined for specific finished goods including the unique options a customer orders. While these bills of materials certainly define the product for production, they have little value when predicting the future.

FIGURE 20

HOIST ARRANGEMENT

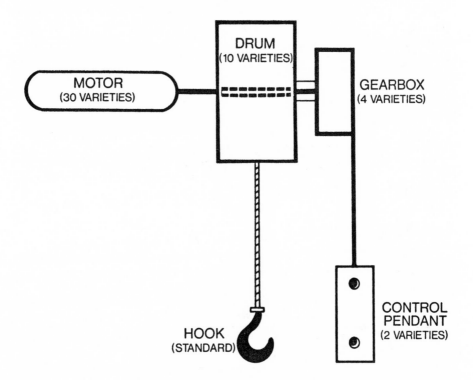

An example of a hoist manufactured from a variety of options is shown in Fig. 20. Five different items, a motor, control pendant, drum, gearbox, and hook, must be assembled together to make a hoist. Customers can select any one of 30 motors, 10 drums, 4 gear boxes, 2 control pendants and the standard hook for their specific hoist. This array of options means there are 2400 uniquely different hoists that could be selected by customers to suit their requirements, simply the multiplication of variables. The company actually produces 50 hoists a week. The minimum master production schedule lead time is 15 weeks from the issuance of a purchase order to procure long lead time items until they have a hoist ready to be shipped to a customer. So it is obviously impossible to predict which 50 out of the 2400 possible finished hoists customers will buy 15 weeks in the future. However, if we focus our attention not on finished hoists but on the major items that are mixed and matched to produce finished hoists, the problem quickly becomes easier. There are only 47 different items that can be selected by customers, which is simply the addition of the variables. Hence forecasting in this case should not be done for finished goods but for the customer selected options, as shown in Fig. 21. The multiplication effect of options on the number of possible finished goods is really seen the day the engineers design an optional hook. Finished goods alternatives jump to 4800 whereas options increment one to 48.

FIGURE 21

PRODUCT DEFINITION
TO IMPROVE FORECASTING

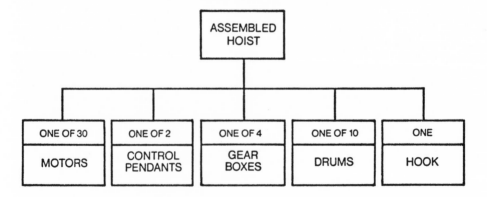

Now let's see how to generate a master production schedule. To start out easily, the master production schedule for the hook assembly is 50/week, simply the total production of all hoists. This could be forecasted certainly 15 weeks into the future and probably further than that depending on the plans for the product family in total. These numbers, exploded through the hook's bill of materials using material requirements planning, will schedule procurement and manufacture of the rough forging, machined forging, swivel, keeper and all other items.

In order of complexity, the next item to plan is the control pendant. As there are two of these, this will not be quite so easy. One way is to use historical sales information to develop a ratio of each control pendant's usage compared to the total sales of hoists. If, historically, 60% of the hoists sold contained the number one control pendant and 40% the number two, then a master production schedule of 30 number one pendants (60% of 50 hoists) and 20 number two pendants could be projected out for 15 weeks, provided the estimate of the future mix of these two items is the same as the historical ratio. This same approach of using historical ratios of sales of individual items within each modular grouping compared to the total sales can be applied to the gear box, drum, and motor options. If it is known that future trends in the mix will differ from history, the master production schedules for future periods can be adjusted to reflect this known change.

Where the motors are concerned, it is possible some are used infrequently because of an unusual voltage or environmental demand. In this case, it could be more logical to plan the infrequently used items using order points or minimum stock levels rather than master scheduling and material requirements planning, or to carry zero stock and quote customers who order these items the lead time to procure, assemble and test hoists using this motor. The decision is a trade-off between predictability of demand, inventory risk and desire to service the customer.

It is important to differentiate clearly here between modular bills of materials and percentage or ratio bills of materials, and their respective master production schedules. Percentage bills of materials will be discussed in detail in the following section but are composite structures containing percentages as the quantity usage figures in the bill of materials. Master production schedules are then for the composite structure, for example hoists, and the percentages in the bill of materials break out plans for the option automatically.

Where modular bills of materials are concerned, master production schedules are provided for each option. Historical sales ratios are used to make these plans, just as with the percentage bill of materials, but this is not done automatically. Human judgement and intervention occurs at the option level with modular bills of materials and at the composite structure level with percentage bills of materials.

In the hoist example, conceptualizing the finished product as modules has improved forecasting the future dramatically. However, it is rare that bills of materials are constructed in a form that isolates or decouples the different modules from one another. Because bills of materials are usually constructed to define finished products, data concerning each option is scattered throughout and is not grouped together. The skill in creating modular bills of materials is to disentangle the options so that separate bills of materials define each option completely.

Some of the toughest items to disentangle are the connecting elements linking one module to another. For example, the electrical cable that joins the control pendant to the gear box has to be included in a bill of materials. If the cable differs based on which specific control pendant is selected, then obviously it belongs in the control pendants' bill of materials. However, if it changes based on the gear box selected then it obviously belongs with the gear boxes. The wire or cable that joins the hook to the drum has to be in a bill of materials. If it is common, it goes in the hook bill of materials. If it is unique to the drum, based on its length to fit a given drum size or type of spooling, then it belongs in the drum bill of materials.

An even tougher proposition is the shaft that links the motor to the gear box. If the design of the shaft is such that the end that connects to the motor is unique depending on which motor is selected, if the length between the gear box and the motor depends on the drum selected, and the end that attaches to the gear box differs based on the gear box selected, 1200 different shaft designs exist. How can these be forecast when only 50 hoists are made each week? If customers will wait the lead time of manufacture of shafts and then assembly of hoists, it's no problem. Just wait for the order. But if for competitive reasons a shorter lead time must be quoted, this particular design would be a problem.

One way out of this dilemma is to have partially machined shafts in inventory that can be finished quickly when the customer's order is received. Another alternative is to standardize the ends of the shaft so only the length is the variable. Still another alternative is to make the shaft from three separate pieces. The end attached to the motor can be configured to suit the motor selected, the end joined to the gear box can be configured to suit the gear box selected, and the length in between made a variable based on the drum selected. These three separate pieces can now be put in their controlling option's bill of materials, and planned in conjunction with all other parts associated with the option.

A tough problem caused by this solution is the probable increase in the standard cost of shafts. However, if 1200 different shaft designs exist, this will cause excessive inventory, poor customer service and factory disruption. It is worthwhile to evaluate when it is better to add direct cost into the product to minimize these problems, an element often missing from value analysis studies.

This logic of designing for flexibility has been picked up by the electronics industry, where many products have redundancy built into them. As a customer's order is booked or a final assembly schedule is issued, those segments of the electronics not required are simply shorted out so they cannot be used. Another good example is automobiles where the body contains many redundant brackets and holes to suit options not always selected. This additional cost of product, minor in many cases, is the penalty paid to provide a high degree of inventory flexibility to produce a product with customer selected options in a very short lead time.

A major problem with this technique, still not addressed, is the predictability of the mix customers will buy in the future. If the mix of options put into the master production schedule differs from what customers actually order, some options will not be available when wanted so some customers will not get their products when needed. At the same time, inventories of the options not sold will grow and the simultaneous objectives of high customer service and low inventories will not be met. In fact, the opposite will occur.

FIGURE 22

PLANNING PRODUCTION

OPTION	HISTORICAL %	MPS	OVERPLAN %	OVERPLAN MPS
HOOK	100	50		
CONTROL PENDANT #1 PENDANT #2	60 40	30 20	70 50	35 25
CONTROL PENDANT TOT	100	50	120	60
GEAR BOX #1				
ETC.				

One way out of this dilemma is to use over-planning, shown in Fig. 22. It means putting more in total in the master production schedule than the theoretical numbers suggest to compensate for inaccurate forecasts of future sales. The extra can be based on intuition, judgement, or actual variability of past sales compared to the average. Of course, the maximum that should be added is what earns a valid return on the extra inventory of options that are likely to be produced.

This extra amount of product can be put into a variety of time periods in the master production schedule. If it is put in the first week, then extra of each module will be made causing on-hand safety stock of each option. If it exists in future time periods, the explosion of bills of materials and lead time off-setting will cause the safety stock to happen at lower levels in the bills of materials, not at the finished option level. The further into the future the over-plan is pushed, the lower down in the bills of materials excess materials will be provided. The trade-offs to consider now are the desired reaction time to customers versus the cost of the extra inventory.

Over-planning the master production schedule allows a variance between actual customer's orders and the forecasted mix to occur without serious consequences. Not over-planning means schedules are based on the theoretical mix, certain to be out of synchronization with actual customer's orders. And when products are not shipped, inventory always grows the fastest. So following the theoretical route will cause excess inventories, poor customer service, and a frantically confused plant trying to change its plans to suit reality.

This now raises a question about a further breakdown of bills of materials to see whether additional improvements are possible. We will use the control pendant as an example. If the two bills of materials were subdivided as shown in Fig. 23 into common parts and parts unique to each pendant, then three bills of materials would now exist where two existed previously. With this grouping, the master production schedule for the common items can be the same as for the hook, that is 50 per week; any over-plan need only be applied to the unique item bills of materials. It is the number of items common versus unique that controls the degree of over-planning that is financially acceptable and earns a valid return. If most of the items are common, then a larger over-plan of the uniques will provide more flexibility in the marketplace; at the same time, inventory investment is significantly reduced.

This further breakdown of bills of materials can improve forecasting the future. For example, if the motors are manufactured by this plant, the disentangling of their bills of materials into common and unique items could take the 30 finished motors and reduce them to a relatively

FIGURE 23

COMMON AND UNIQUES

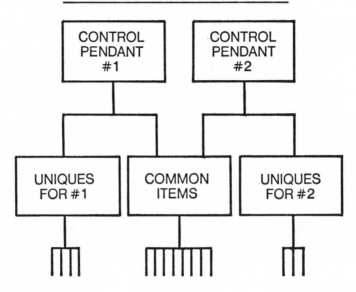

few unique groupings of items depending on the differences between various motors. If most differences are voltage or speed, then the manufacturing process can make different motors from essentially common raw materials. If the difference is for environmental conditions, then separate bill of material groupings will be needed for the external casings of the motor to provide these environmental characteristics.

An extension of this way of structuring is to group all common parts, together with the hook, into one large "common" bill of materials; the unique parts for each option still exist in their option bills of materials. Although this suits product planning and simplifies the job of master production scheduling, it does not suit creating manufacturing instructions to build the options. Complex coding will be necessary to identify which parts in the large common bill of materials go with each option so assembly bills of materials can be made.

A better way of structuring is to make separate bills of materials for the common items in each option group, making it easier to merge these with the parts unique to a given option to make bills of materials that define the product. Sometimes there are large numbers of option groups and hence a large number of bills of materials are needed to define common part groupings. Fig. 24 shows one way to minimize the master production scheduling job at the same time as common groupings are identified with their pertinent option group. Here a "super common" bill of materials is created which includes each option common grouping. One master production schedule can be made for the "super common" item without destroying the ability to make finished product bills of materials.

This approach raises two significant questions that must be addressed. The first is how far down the bill of materials should this regrouping of items be done. As bills of materials are disentangled and regrouped differently, this improves predicting the future but makes it more difficult to format documents to instruct the factory how to make the product or to allow the engineer to see clearly how the product is constructed. Generally, restructuring of bills of materials should be done at the highest level possible. Only when there are significant additional benefits should lower levels be disentangled, simply because of the problems of recombining the option groups back into complete bills of materials again.

The second area of concern is the design of products to enable restructuring and grouping to occur. Without significant pressure on the engineers to design for cost, function and the ability to create valid master production schedules, the products will not be amenable to the modularizing process. Hence, low cost, quality products will not be made on time to suit customer demands.

FIGURE 24

SUPER COMMON BoM

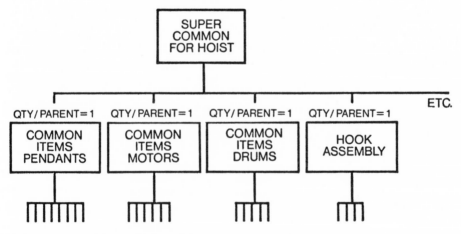

Referring back to the control pendant as an example, if pendant number one has one up and one down button but pendant number two has up, down, and emergency stop buttons, then the two boxes could be different—a small box for number one and a larger one for number two. The top cover now must be different. The cables hooking the control boxes to the motor and braking systems could have different numbers of wires. The only common items in this case are the up and down buttons with everything else unique. However, with the concept of modularity and the need to create valid master production schedules as key design objectives, one control box will be specified large enough for either the number one or number two configurations. The cables connecting pendants to gear boxes will be identical with some wires redundant for the number one box. The front panels of the boxes will be identical with a plug button for the hole if the emergency stop is not selected. This means everything in the bills of materials for control pendants will be common except for the plug button for pendant number one and the additional switch for pendant number two. With this configuration, only very low inventories are necessary to provide high customer service. As mentioned earlier, though, this approach has to be carefully analyzed to ensure reductions in inventory and improvements in customer service can pay for the increased costs. This analysis is not done as well in most plants as it should be.

Computer programs can be written to assist in restructuring bills of materials already loaded in a computer. But the skill is to design new products and structure their bills of materials to suit forecasting and master production scheduling right from the start. However, if existing bills of materials have been loaded into the computer and now they must be evaluated for restructuring purposes, programs that take a variety of bills of materials and compare them can be useful. These programs compare selected bills of materials and identify all common ingredients. The unique items are identified to their specific product bills of materials.

This could be a first step in the disentangling process. However, a few key people familiar with the product, the needs of the market place, and the design implications, can usually do this job more effectively than utilizing computerized systems. The advantage of people doing this job is they will see many opportunities to improve the design as they do their analysis, which is not possible if the computer does it. And because of the need to design and structure products correctly when new products are designed, using key people to evaluate existing designs teaches them how to design new products in a manner to suit all needs.

Generic Coding/Menu Selection

Whenever bill of material restructuring discussions take place, the question is always raised whether these "new" bills of materials are in addition to the regular ones. As mentioned in Chapter 4, it is important to differentiate between what is in a computer's files and what is printed out in a given format. When modular groupings are put in a computer it is often possible to format finished product reports simply by linking the option and common groupings together.

One way to do this is to use "generic coding" or "menu selection" techniques as shown in Fig. 25 for the hoist. One menu is required for each family of hoists. All available options are listed under their option group heading. As a unique hoist is specified, either in order entry to suit a customer request or in manufacturing to suit an assembly authorization, the decision matrix suggested by the menu selection technique must be followed. The bottom line of the chart says this is a model 640 hoist which links to all items common to this family of hoists; in our example, only the hook assembly is common. If a second hook was available, then selecting model 640 would not link to any bill of materials within the system. The first question is "What control pendant is re-

FIGURE 25

HOIST MENU MODEL 640

ITEM A — CONTROL PENDANT

WITHOUT EMER. STOP (1)
WITH EMER. STOP (2)

ITEM C — DRUM

25 FT CAPACITY (1)
50 FT CAPACITY (2)
75 FT CAPACITY (3)
100 FT CAPACITY (4)

ITEM B — GEAR BOX

10 FT/MIN LINE SPEED (1)
20 FT/MIN LINE SPEED (2)
50 FT/MIN LINE SPEED (3)
100 FT/MIN LINE SPEED (4)

ITEM D — MOTOR

WITHOUT BRAKE — 240 V 60 Hz (1)
WITHOUT BRAKE — 440 V 60 Hz (2)
WITHOUT BRAKE — 550 V 60 Hz (3)
WITH BRAKE — 240 V 60 Hz (4)
ETC.

640   A __2__   B __1__   C __3__   D __4__

quired, with or without emergency brake?" Item A picks up the common items for either control pendant. The number inserted next to Item A picks up the unique bill of materials to go with the common items to build a particular control pendant. Obviously, further selections of gear box, drum, and motor, cause a mixing and matching of common and unique items to produce a configured hoist.

The ability to make an assembly bill of materials from this menu selection technique is affected by exactly where restructuring occurred in the bill of materials. If the modularity occurs high up in the bill of materials and all at the same level, the common parts can be grouped easily with the unique parts. A line sequence or similar sequence coding method allows the bill of materials to be printed for each option. The assembly or engineering people can use this just as if a complete product bill of materials had been in the computer. If the modularity is low down in the bills of materials or exists at different levels for each option grouping, then additonal structures will probably be required in the computer to generate this information.

One problem with the menu approach is costing the product when the routing and labor standards change based on which options are selected to make a unique configuration. In this case, the routing has to be structured similar to modular bills of materials. A common routing for all products is needed with optional operations or standards selected as the product options are selected. Hence, the routing will be built up in much the same way as the bill of materials, allowing finished products to be costed and specific routing instructions issued to the plant.

The modular bill of materials is the most flexible way of serving all users if the product design suits this particular treatment. Master production schedules can be created for each unique option and the common groupings, and customers promised delivery based on their availability. A changing mix forecasted for unique options to occur over the next year, for instance a move to more emergency stops on hoists because of Occupational Safety and Health Act (OSHA) regulations, can be put into the master production schedule simply by slowly increasing the amount of number two pendants in the master production schedule and decreasing the number ones. Picking lists, assembly instructions, product costing and the other uses of bills of materials can be easily accommodated.

Its success, however, is based on a clear understanding by all functional groups of the underlying goals of this type of bill of materials. The sales department must understand that if they wish flexibility in the market place, they must spend a lot of time defining the options they wish to offer customers and in making sure they spend this time early in the design of a new product. Adding new options at a later time may require the bill of materials to be completely restructured to include them, and possibly cause the basic design to be invalid to achieve their objectives.

Engineers must understand that along with their goals of designing products to perform a function at minimum cost, they must also design them to give maximum customer service with minimum inventory. Financial people must agree that sometimes additional extra costs in the product are worthwhile to reduce inventories and improve service. Far too many excellent, well-designed modular products have been destroyed by value analysis teams proving they can save significant standard cost dollars, but in so doing, causing dramatic increases in inventory and significant drop-offs in customer service.

Percentage or Ratio Bills

This bill of materials contains product structures where the quantity is a percent of usage of an item relative to the parent part. One way of explaining this is to use the hoist described earlier under modular bills of materials. A percentage bill of materials constructed for the hoist is shown as Fig. 26. In this case, the percent of usage that was used in the modular bill of materials to construct specific master production schedules

FIGURE 26

HOIST PERCENTAGE BoM

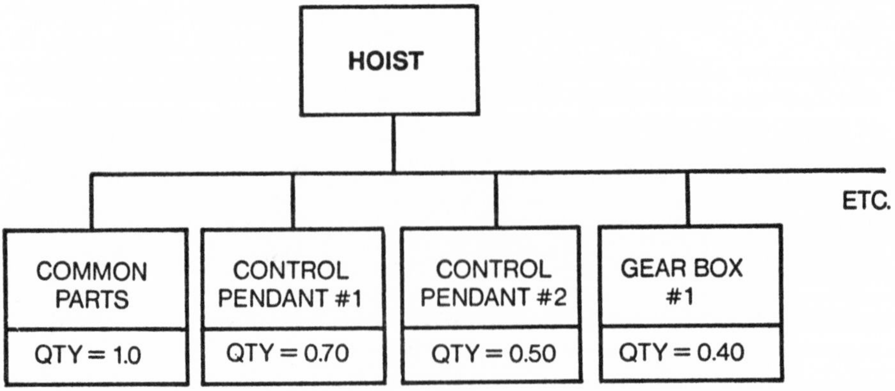

for each module has now been built into a ratio bill of materials. Using this technique, the master production schedule can simply be 50 hoists per week and the computer explosion through the percentage will get the mix of items planned at lower levels to suit this mix configuration.

A variation on this technique is sometimes called a "super bill of materials". This term is normally used when a variety of *finished* products are put into a percentage bill of materials for the product family. It is used by companies with a wide variety of end products and no modularity. One example is a window manufacturer making hundreds of different sizes and colors of finished windows within each product family. They have bills of materials for each finished window and these are grouped into a super bill of materials for the product family. Historical sales provide the percentages.

Another way of creating a percentage bill of materials is to only list the raw materials in a product. An example is an electric motor manufacturer mainly producing special motors. They cannot manufacture parts or motors until the customer order is received and the design specified by engineering. However, the motors are made from a fairly limited number of raw materials, such as bar stock for shafts, steel sheet for laminations and rough castings. All similar items are grouped together, for instance all end bracket castings, and the quantities for these common raw materials grouped together based on the historical mix of sales

FIGURE 27

RAW MATERIAL RATIO BoM

NAME: 250 NEMA FRAME BRACKET ROUGH CASTINGS

PART NO.	HISTORICAL USAGE	QUANTITY PER
39765	1806	.955
40249	1683	.892
10762	97	.051
59327	89	.047
83596	69	.036
35962	34	.018
TOTAL	3778	2.002

as well as future booked orders. An example of this bill of materials is shown in Fig. 27. The unique part of this bill of materials is there are two brackets per motor, hence the straight percent of usage must be doubled. Similar bills of materials exist for all other raw material categories needed to produce a motor.

The percentage bill of materials is a very mixed bag. It has some strong features but some very negative ones as well. It should be used with great caution and only after thorough understanding of its strengths and weaknesses.

It is best used where the percentages simply convert a family master production schedule into detailed master production schedules for a large number of modules or end items. This is sometimes called a two level master production schedule. The key point, though, is that the real master production schedule driving the manufacturing control system is the lower of the two, not the family schedule. The percentages simply reduce the amount of information being massaged manually to create this lower schedule.

This contrasts with the use of percentages in bills of materials where the master production schedule is for the family or parent item and material requirements planning creates the detailed schedules. In other words, there is no lower level master production schedule, just the one at the top. The discussion in the rest of this section applies to this use of percentages.

The percentage bill of materials is effective where the historical mix is very constant over time or where a large part of the future has been sold and the actual needed configurations specified. One example is again the window manufacturer, where the historical mix of end items in each product family is constant year-to-year with very minor changes. They use the percentage bill of materials in their master production schedule starting in week 4. This tells them what hardware, glass and finished wooden components are needed to produce the standard mix of windows. Customer's orders fill up the first three weeks of the master production schedule; production can make any short-term adjustments necessary to react to this specific mix within the lead time of three weeks. Cushions are provided through over-planning in the fourth week to have additional parts and components in stock. Key vendors also carry inventories of parts which can be ordered into the factory quickly. This provides the needed flexibility to react to unexpected orders in the short-range.

For those not so fortunate to have a stable mix of product, the problems start to escalate. A percentage quantity introduced into a bill of materials must be maintained. Hence, some way of evaluating history and updating the percentages regularly must be provided. Some companies have automated maintenance and the computer adjusts these percentages periodically. Others simply review historical information and update the percentages manually. As these numbers are changed, though, material requirements planning changes the requirements at all levels in the bills of materials and frequently generates excessive nervousness within the factory and with vendor schedules.

If it is known that the mix of items will change in the future, it is very difficult to reflect this future change in the planning process. How can the quantities in the bills of materials reflect these future changes other than in the current time period? There are some effectivity management systems that manage quantities in bills of materials, but these are rarities and not normal in manufacturing control software packages. Without this capability, a known shift in mix can only be handled by a variety of bills of materials each containing different percentages tied to specific time periods.

Sometimes companies produce products with seasonal sales patterns. In the low season, they want to produce those items that store the maximum amount of capacity with the smallest amount of purchased material in the smallest cube with the lowest risk of obsolescence. In the peak season, the mix they produce is those items containing the least amount of capacity with the highest risk of obsolescence. The amount of purchased material and cube is not a factor at this time. A percentage bill of materials will have great difficulty keeping up with these on-going production mix changes.

Quoting customer deliveries based on the specific consumption of options becomes a little more difficult with a percentage bill of materials. Referring back to the hoist percentage bill of materials in Fig. 26, if 40 hoists have been sold out of 50 scheduled in a given week, leaving 10 left to be sold, and a customer's order arrives for 10 more, can this order be promised for that week? An analysis of which specific options are still available has to be made. The fact that there are 10 hoists unsold does not necessarily mean the mix of options available matches the average usage or the next 10 specific customer's orders. This means the order promising route is complicated by having to explode customers orders into their detail parts to check for the "gating" items.

Duplication of structures is necessary when percentage bills of materials are used, unless they are the super bill of materials variety mentioned earlier. Specific finished product bills of materials are required to support financial, manufacturing and engineering people, so redundancy and duplication has to occur, causing problems with engineering change control and dual maintenance features.

This technique has most value when a significant early portion of the master production schedule has been sold. Specific bills of materials have replaced the percentage bill of materials for this horizon. The percentage bill of materials fills out the longer range portion of the master production schedule. Material requirements planning, exploded through the percentages, only serves to plan and schedule long lead time raw materials. If the raw materials are unique to finished products, then procuring the right unique materials is difficult unless the percentages are very stable over time. The percentage bill of materials may or may not do this adequately. With common raw materials the approach is excellent.

Percentages are also useful in companies with a large number of options or finished products that must be master production scheduled and the sheer volume of these prohibits using the modular approach or any other detailed technique. The penalties of percentages are then outweighed by the benefits of dependant planning and the management value of a master production schedule. The choice becomes one of working the details or playing the percentages.

Over-planning can occur two ways with percentage bills of materials. One way is to inflate the percentages to more than the historical average usage and the other is simply to bump the master production schedule quantity in a given time bucket.

Inflating the percentages allows contingency to be applied to specific options as their unique variability of demand suggests. However, this means maintenance of a lot of detailed numbers, it probably does not foster marketing intelligence applied to the future as it is too detailed, and nervousness in lower level plans will occur as changes are made.

Bumping the master production schedule gives equal over-planning to all options, theoretically incorrect, but it does make this decision highly visible. It can be managed and reviewed at high management levels, and does not have the same tendency to generate nervous schedules.

The selection of which method to use must be based on a clear understanding of the products and their demand patterns, as well as the cost and risk of planning excess inventories as safety stock.

Inverted Bills

A single commodity, such as tape, aspirin, and photographic film, can be converted into many unique products. The way this bulk commodity is configured or packaged through the final production process makes this large variety of end items. An example is the magnetic tape shown in Fig. 28. The coated jumbo roll of tape is made first and then slit and further processed into a wide variety of lengths, widths, quality ratings and packaging—the items customers buy. If finished products are forecasted and master production scheduled, because of the variability of sales of each finished product, the quality of the master production schedule becomes questionable. These questionable numbers then exploded through traditional bills of materials provide questionable information for the bulk commodity.

The most logical place to forecast and master production schedule these items is at the bulk product level, for example, magnetic tape in a jumbo roll. Aggregate sales demand at the jumbo level, simply because of the reduction in mathematics and statistics, is much more reliable. However, if this is where the master production schedule is created, all the ingredients for the jumbo will be planned correctly using the normal

FIGURE 28

MAGNETIC TAPE BoM

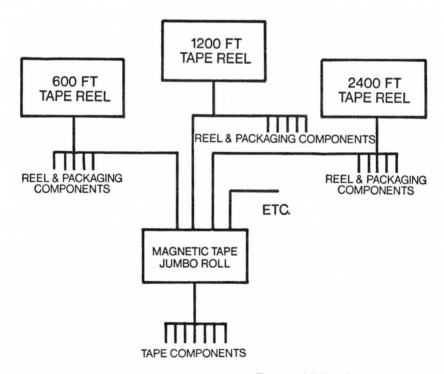

explosion logic of material requirements planning. But plans will not be generated for the packaging materials and reels needed to make specific end items.

One approach is to use modular bills of materials where reels and packaging are treated as options to the basic jumbo configuration. Another approach is to use percentage bills of materials that are upside down. Shown in Fig. 29, packaging groups are linked as components to the jumbo film. From a strictly engineering standpoint, this bill of materials is ridiculous; you do not need packaging to produce a jumbo roll of film. But for planning purposes, tieing packaging groups to the jumbo roll can be very effective. It retains dependent relationships; a master production schedule plans all components needed. If the master production schedule for jumbo rolls is increased or decreased, the schedules for reels and packaging materials are also changed proportionally.

The assumption with the inverted bill of materials, as with all percentage bills of materials, is that the percent of usage is relatively constant and predictable. Contingency can be put into the plan by inflating the percentages or by increasing the master production schedule for jumbo rolls, as discussed in the percentage bill of materials section. In this example, increasing the master production schedule is unlikely to be the right approach because the variables in question are the reels and packaging, and it is only these areas that need contingency.

One of the serious drawbacks to this approach is it will force signifi-

FIGURE 29

INVERTED BoM

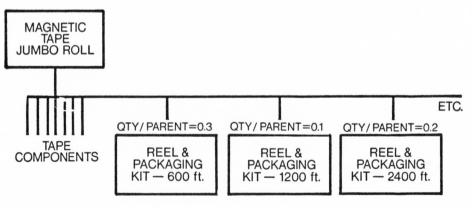

cant redundancy into the files defining bills of materials. These bills of materials cannot be used by cost accountants, engineers, or as a customer specification. A bill of materials for each specific end product is needed along with the inverted structures.

The advantage is simply that the master production scheduling activity is best at the product family level. The inverted bill of materials allows dependencies to be used when planning and many different finished goods can be planned quickly with just one number in the master production schedule. It cannot be used for promising customer deliveries unless a detailed analysis of available material is made.

Add/Delete

Many companies make minor modifications to standard products to suit the specific needs of each customer or to provide a wide variety of finished goods from a fairly standard product design. One way of defining the specials is to use one basic bill of materials as the standard and simply identify which parts are to be removed and which parts added to this basic bill of materials to make a new configuration. Many computer programs provide the facility to retrieve an existing bill of materials from the files, add and delete items to it, and hence create a complete new bill of materials for the item being designed.

An add/delete bill of materials does not create brand new bills of materials each time but simply stores within the computer the additions and subtractions from the basic bill of materials. This is called an "add/delete", a "same as except", or a "comparative" bill of materials, as shown in Fig. 30. The basic product "A" has a complete bill of materials defining its make-up. The new product "A_1" has a bill of materials with only the differences and this data is stored in the computer this way.

From a bill of materials maintenance standpoint as well as in the factory, this is a convenient technique. If the basic machine is made frequently, so most people know how it goes together, telling the production people which parts to omit and which parts to add to make the new product makes factory documentation very easy. It is certainly easier than providing a complete bill of materials for each new finished product and everybody having to read through it to find the differences. However, this positive aspect is completely outweighed by the negative aspects of trying to use such a bill of materials in a planning system.

First, inaccuracy can occur much easier with a comparative than with a complete bill of materials. For example, when the comparative bill of materials is entered into the computer, editing routines can

FIGURE 30

ADD/DELETE BoM

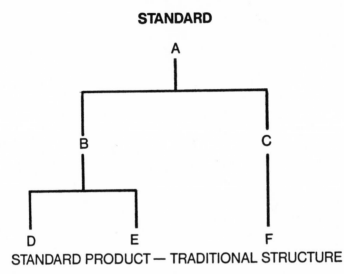

STANDARD

STANDARD PRODUCT — TRADITIONAL STRUCTURE

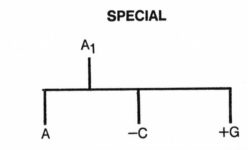

SPECIAL

SPECIAL PRODUCT — ADD/DELETE STRUCTURE

check that the parts with negative quantities do exist in the basic bill of materials and the parts being added are not duplicating parts already there. However, it is more difficult to prevent the engineer from incorrectly changing the basic bill of materials sometime later. He could delete an item the add and delete bill of materials assumes is there and is already planning to remove. This problem is shown in Fig. 31 for product A and A1 of Fig. 30. Part C was removed from the standard bill of materials and replaced with H. The negative C was not made negative H. If this change is made, then the planning for both item C and H is wrong. Too much is being planned for one part (H) and the item that carries the negative quantity (C), has total requirements below what may be needed for all other products. One company that used this technique found when they tried to calculate standard costs for their products us-

FIGURE 31

ADD/DELETE BoM ERROR

STANDARD

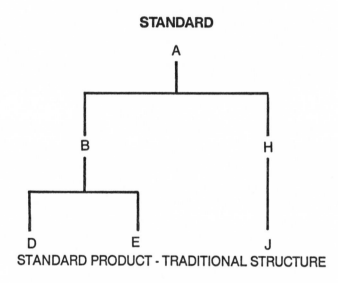

STANDARD PRODUCT - TRADITIONAL STRUCTURE

SPECIAL

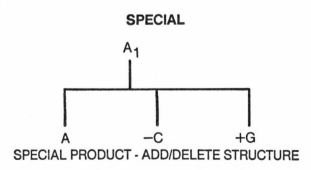

SPECIAL PRODUCT - ADD/DELETE STRUCTURE

ing the computer bills of materials that many items were overcosted because of these kinds of errors and other items ended up with negative standard costs. The financial people in this company are still trying to figure out whether to buy or sell items that have a negative standard cost to make a profit!

The second problem is with the computer planning logic. When the modified product is scheduled, standard material requirements planning logic assumes you plan to take a standard product out of inventory and actually modify it to suit the new configuration. However, add and delete bills of materials rarely indicate the basic product should be physically modified. They are created to modify the standard bill of materials only from a definition standpoint. Hence, additional logic is required in material requirements planning so that inventories of standard finished goods must be ignored. One company solved this problem by creating an additional part number, a pseudo number, for all standard products, which had by definition zero on-hand, zero safety stock, and zero lead time. The part number for standard products was simply linked one for one to this pseudo number. Modifications to the standard product were not made to its real part number but to the pseudo number, as shown in Fig. 32.

The third problem is to get the negative and their corresponding plus quantities to line up in a given time bucket. Material requirements planning plans items in the future. The positive and negative numbers in the bills of materials must line up in a future period to give a net zero requirement. However, the lead times for planning standard and modified products can be different. Even if they are the same, material requirements planning could plan the components for different time buckets. See Fig. 33. Many material requirements planning software packages do not handle negative quantities showing up as the requirements. They give completely wrong planning outputs with this data.

One way of solving this is to use the pseudo number mentioned in the previous paragraph, where by definition the basic item must have zero lead time. However, this forces the add and delete activities to only occur one level down in the bill of materials. If items several levels down in the bill of materials are added and deleted, the same problem of lead time differences will occur, upsetting the planning process disastrously.

The fourth problem is the inability to provide adequate over-planning. If the basic item is fairly predictable but the special finished product is highly variable, it will be important to over-plan the unique components used in the special product. If the special product number is over-planned, the standard product will be over-planned as well, causing excess inventories where they are not needed. Even if this bill of materi-

FIGURE 32

ADD/DELETE BoM WITH PSEUDO

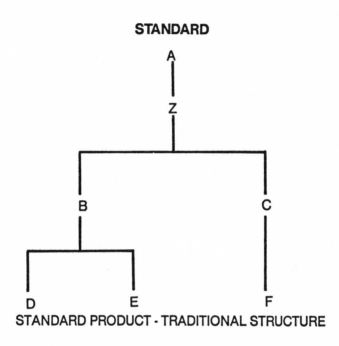

STANDARD

STANDARD PRODUCT - TRADITIONAL STRUCTURE

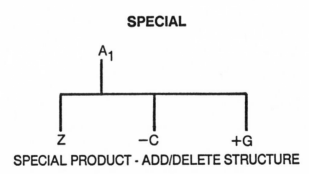

SPECIAL

SPECIAL PRODUCT - ADD/DELETE STRUCTURE

als is used with an optional product configuration, as shown in Fig. 34, over-planning the option with the negative quantity increases the deductions from the basic product. The total number of parts always remains

FIGURE 33

TIMING ADDS AND DELETES

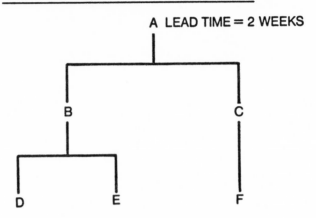

A LEAD TIME = 2 WEEKS

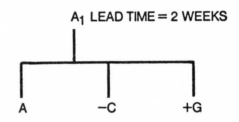

A_1 LEAD TIME = 2 WEEKS

WEEK NUMBER	1	2	3	4	5	6	7	8	9	10
MASTER PRODUCTION SCHEDULE FOR A_1										5
MATERIAL REQUIREMENTS FOR A								5		
MATERIAL REQUIREMENTS FOR C						+5		-5		

the same. This reduces the planning on the standard part below the expected needs with equally disastrous results. A much better approach is to create add-only modular bills of materials for each option. A no-clock option bill of materials, for example, should be provided which will contain the blank plate; the blank plate should be removed from the basic automobile and the option bill of materials should only contain the clock.

FIGURE 34

ADD/DELETE WITH OVERPLANNING

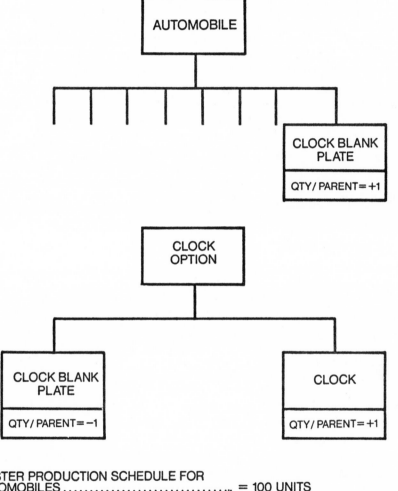

MASTER PRODUCTION SCHEDULE FOR
AUTOMOBILES............................... = 100 UNITS

CLOCK OPTIONS AT 40% (HISTORY)... ...... = 40 UNITS

OVERPLANNING FOR CLOCK OPTIONS AT 10% = 10 UNITS

PLANNING FOR CLOCKS...................... = 50 UNITS (HISTORY PLUS)
CONTINGENCY)

PLANNING FOR BLANK PLATES .... = 50 UNITS (10 SHORT BASED
ON HISTORY)

Therefore, adequate over-planning or contingency planning can be applied to those items expected to have highly variable demands.

The fifth problem is the master production schedule has to be made at the end item level because only end item bills of materials exist. Depending on their number and the amount of uniqueness between them, this may or may not give a valid master production schedule. As actual customer's orders are booked differing from the master production schedule, considerable disruption will occur throughout the plant trying to deliver special products to customers on time. Significant safety stock applied to unique items throughout the bill of materials is the only way to compensate for this lack of planning ability at the master production schedule level, giving unmatched sets of safety stocks and hence significant inventories of components.

If the add and delete technique is used it should modify a standard bill of materials into a complete reconfigured bill of materials. This will eliminate most of the problems mentioned earlier, except the difficulty of creating valid master production schedules for many finished products.

Family Bills

Most companies create bills of materials to define specific finished products, either using modules or by making a specific bill of materials for a given end item. A few companies construct bills of materials that define a *family* of end products. In Chapter 5, zoning the master production schedule and the needs for each of the zones to generate limited specific information was discussed. Significant improvements in master production scheduling, and hence better scheduling of the right materials at the right time can occur by using a bill of materials for a family of products rather than for specific end items, especially for the long-range portions of the master production schedule. This was already shown for one kind of product in Fig. 27.

Fig. 35 shows a family bill of materials for a truck axle made from a housing, gears, shafts, wheels, and brakes. The configured axle may be unique to a given truck manufacturer. However, lower down the bill of materials, these items become raw materials, for example, housing castings, gear forging blanks and axle shaft material. If these materials are common to a wide variety of finished axles then there is no requirement to make finished axle master production schedules for the long range, only for the total family. The family bill of materials used in the far out master production schedule horizon provides all the information necessary to procure the right raw materials.

FIGURE 35

AXLE FAMILY BILL OF MATERIAL

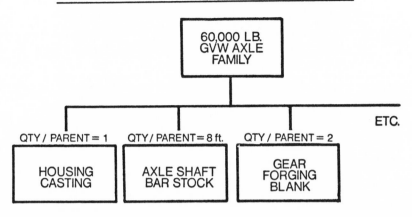

Taking this logic one step further, if the lead time to procure some raw materials is covered by customers' orders for specific axles, then only the long lead time items not covered by these orders need be in the family bill of materials. These are the only items that must be ordered prior to receipt of a customer's order for a finished axle. A lead time offset bill of materials is shown in Fig. 36, depicting the time horizons needed to produce an axle assembly. This bill of material is in essence an indented bill of material, the indentation amount the lead time for each item. With a time scale across the bottom, it is easy to see when each item in a bill of materials is needed in relation to the completion date of the end product.

For example, the housing casting is needed five weeks before the completion date of the axle assembly. But the housing casting has a five-week lead time, so it has to be ordered ten weeks prior to the axle completion date.

If a customer order book of six weeks is maintained, then only the items with lead times beyond those orders, i.e. the housing casting, bearings and machined wheels, need be in the family bill of materials. The timing of real need for these parts will not be exactly correct with this bill of materials, but this will probably be compensated for by the improved quality of the master production schedule. A computer program that shows this lead time build up for products can suggest how to construct family bills of materials to improve master production schedules. This is a worthwhile addition to every company's bill of materials reports.

It may be possible at this point to combine product families into a

FIGURE 36

LEAD TIME OFFSET AXLE BoM

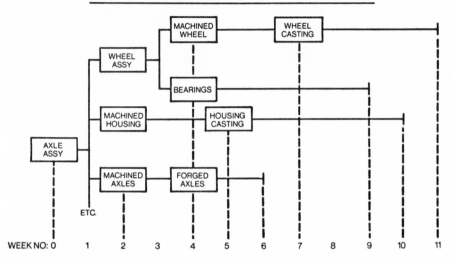

larger product family because the long lead time items may be common to several product groups. With this bill of materials in the planning system, the master production scheduling activity in the far out zones becomes a relatively simple exercise. As these zones are far into the future, some contingency planning should be applied. Over-planning the master production schedule for the family will generate larger stocks of these long lead time materials. This is the inventory with least value added, providing flexibility to change the mix in the master production schedule in the short-range to support actual customers' orders as they are booked.

The negative to this technique is that in most cases it generates additional structures in the bill of materials file simply to support the planning group. However, these bills of materials are also of value to foster use of standard materials, or to show where to reduce the stacked lead times, both worthwhile objectives. The more standard the raw materials and the shorter their lead time, the more likely right materials will be available at the right time to suit actual customers' orders.

Selecting the Right Bill of Materials Format

A number of different ways of looking at the structure of bills of materials have been presented in this chapter. Fig. 37 recaps the strengths

FIGURE 37

BoM STRUCTURE COMPARISON

CHARACTERISTIC　　BoM TYPE	MODULAR	PERCENTAGE	INVERTED	ADD/ DELETE	FAMILY
FORECAST QUALITY	GOOD	GOOD	GOOD	BAD	GOOD
OVERPLANNING	YES	YES	YES	NO	YES
DUPLICATE STRUCTURES	NO[2]	YES	YES	NO	YES
RESTRUCTURING EFFORT	HIGH	MEDIUM	MEDIUM	LOW	HIGH
REDESIGN EFFORT	HIGH	LOW	LOW	LOW	MED.
TIME PHASED MIX CHANGES	YES	NO	NO	YES	NO
MARKETING INPUTS	HIGH	LOW	LOW	HIGH	LOW
MASTER PROD. SCHED. EFFORT	HIGH	LOW	LOW	HIGH	LOW
HANDLE SEASONALITY	YES	NO	NO	YES	NO
CUSTOMER DELIVERY PROMISES	GOOD	BAD[1]	BAD[1]	BAD	GOOD

1　Can be made good with two-level master production schedule for options.

2　There may be some redundancy depending on the product and its design, usually low in volume.

and weaknesses of each approach. Focus must be on the primary objective when creating different bill of materials groupings, which is the ability to plan the future in the best possible way and create a valid master production schedule. The objective must include the opportunity to provide contingency to take care of expected deviations of actual customer bookings from the plan.

The product being considered has a significant impact on which bill of materials grouping is the best to achieve the above objective. And different groupings can be used at the same time on the same product. For example, a company with a huge variety of customer selected options could use the modular approach for the high cost, long lead time items and a percentage bill of materials for the remaining low cost, short lead time items. This way, over-planning can be applied carefully to the high cost items and customer delivery promises made considering these items' schedules in detail. The percentage bill of materials containing the low cost, short lead time items can have a large over-plan quantity; this will generate adequate contingency to prevent these items from holding up customer's orders without causing excessive inventories. The key point is skilled people from various functions working together on this problem must develop the best bill of materials structure or structures to be used for the products being considered.

It is interesting that whenever these approaches are used, the design of the product is seen as the limiting factor in predicting the future well. As soon as this is recognized and accepted, ways of improving the design, not from a functional standpoint but from a predictive standpoint, becomes a worthwhile goal. As soon as changes are made to standardize products and standard modules are used wherever possible, improved master production schedules provide more of the right inventory to service customers, which makes return on investment, the primary measure of a company's management, improve significantly.

7   Engineering Changes and Effectivity Management

Engineering changes are the bane of manufacturing people. Because a change disturbs the status quo, it is reacted to negatively and the people initiating the change become the butt of sarcastic comments. Yet change is a necessity in the technologically demanding world we live in, so we should not resist change but accept it readily. The costs involved, though, demand that tight controls be exercised over the implementation of changes to ensure the least amount of problems and maximum amount of gain.

Engineering changes fall into five basic groupings:

1. Mandatory change immediately. No further production allowed under the old configuration.
2. Implement the change as soon as possible.
3. Implement the change on a specific date, or at a given product serial number.
4. Implement in the most cost effective way, considering inventory levels, tooling and phase in costs.
5. Temporary deviation.

There are many concerns when an engineering change is proposed, such as who is authorized to make this change, who has the responsibility to review and comment on it, who will be charged with any obsoleted materials and tooling, new tooling procurement or other costs of making the change, and how to implement the change efficiently. From a bills of materials standpoint, the major problems are how to implement the change correctly through the production scheduling and material planning system, how to support spare parts for the old design, and how to record the product design before and after the change because of governmental regulations, spare parts documentation, product liability considerations, or simply as a historical record of the product's design.

Causes of Change

Mandatory Change. A mandatory change is usually because of a defect significant enough to hurt a product's position in the marketplace, in extreme cases because it endangers human life, because of a new government regulation, or simply the customer's desire. There is rarely much discussion in a company over the necessity for a mandatory change.

Implement as soon as possible. The reasons for this change can be similar to a mandatory change except this change has a lower urgency. For example, a product defect is not so significant as to stop production but significant enough to want to correct the defect quickly. Other reasons could be because of severe problems in manufacturing or problems procuring to the old design or because of large cost reductions available with the new design.

Implement at a specific point in time. This type of change is to coincide with an event, such as one contract ending and a new one starting, or to suit a major product model revision, such as the annual model change-over in the automobile industry. In most cases, these events are known well ahead of time, so the planning for change can be well coordinated.

Implement at least cost. The majority of reasons for this change are because of minor improvements in function, cost reductions or ease of manufacture. The emphasis is to achieve implementation with the smallest impact on the business.

Some of the alternatives that need evaluating to decide when to implement are: "Is it cheaper to throw away some materials if the new process is less expensive or to process all old materials first? What spare parts will be needed and should an extra amount of the old item be produced on the last production run to supply several years of spare parts needs? Will any new tooling required be available in time to produce the new item before all old items are used up? Is the existing tooling going to be modified to make the new part and if so when can the old tooling be released for the modification process? What about the capacity implications of making the change? Will more capacity from specific resources be needed for the new item and will it be available? What are the total costs of making this change and is it worthwhile making?" All these questions and more must be asked about these kinds of engineering changes to define implementation dates and the validity of the change.

Temporary deviation. These are almost always triggered by manufacturing or procurement problems. If the right parts are not available or cannot be made available for a while, for either vendor or production problems, or there is a desire to use up some potentially obsolete material on this product, then the temporary deviation is used to start and stop production of this alternate part.

Engineering Change Review.

The intricacies of successfully introducing change into a manufacturing plant usually cause the establishment of an engineering change review board. Their charter varies from plant to plant but usually is based on the following:

Should the change be made at all? This is normally not a consideration with mandatory changes or when the pressure for change comes from external influences such as the customer. But if the change is internally generated, the review board performs the function of screening out all unjustified or uneconomic modifications. Without this audit many trivial changes are implemented, causing delays, confusion and costs way in excess of any benefits.

When is the best timing? Again, this is not a consideration with mandatory, immediate changes. However, all other types of changes need careful planning to make sure the change is implemented at the most feasible time. To arrive at the best timing, consideration must be taken of current inventory levels of the old parts and materials, availability of new parts and materials, spare parts needs for the old item, tooling changes, and upcoming factory schedules.

Cost allocations. This will be discussed in more detail later in this chapter. Suffice it to say here that all costs for making changes must be allocated to an existing budget. This can be a politically explosive issue, so the cost allocation is often a function of the review board.

Schedule follow-up. After a change is planned and scheduled, the change review board monitors progress and ensures the change is implemented on target.

Information dissemination. The people who must be notified about a change vary depending on the change itself. The board functions as a clearing house to ensure all affected parties are aware of each change and its expected implementation schedule.

It is a rare business that handles changes well without a review board meeting on a regular schedule. The make-up of this group varies from plant to plant but permanent members usually come from design engineering, production control, manufacturing and accounting. Ad hoc members are usually drawn from purchasing, sales, and quality control.

It must be emphasized that changes are a source of significant profits or losses. An uncontrolled environment of change will be expensive. The costs will not show up in any one place but will be buried in manufacturing variances, obsolete inventory write-offs, year end physical inventory differences and loss of productivity in the plant. A controlled environment will let only the cost effective changes through, and will help implement these changes with minimal upset and disruption.

Effectivity Management

Before starting a discussion of the ways of implementing changes, the first item is to decide what constitutes a change from a bills of materials point of view. Many engineering changes are informational in nature hence do not affect the part numbers and their structural relationships. Such things as additional notes on drawings to help clarify the pictorial view fall into this category. But sometimes the part or assembly itself is modified. Here is where the distinction of change and its affect on the bills of materials becomes grey.

The best way to determine when a bill of materials must change is if a part number must change. If the modification to a part does not change its fit, form or function (engineering terms), it is completely interchangeable with the old part; therefore, the part number need not change so the bill of materials need not change. An example could be an adjustment to the tolerances of a dimension.

If the modification to the part makes it non-interchangeable, then its part number must change. (Some companies avoid changing the part number by advancing a revision letter suffix to the part number. Of course, to a planning system this is still a part number change so all references to the part must include the correct revision letter.) As soon as the part number changes, then its bill of materials, if it has one, and the bill of materials of its parent assembly must change. The laws of fit, form, and function then apply to the parent assembly to see if its part number must change. If the part change has not affected the interchangeability of the parent, then the parent part number need not change. However, if it is now non-interchangeable, then its part number must change and *its* parents' bill of materials must change. The laws of fit, form and function are applied at each level in the bills of materials until either an interchangeable condition is found or a brand new top level identifier is created.

There are a variety of ways of notifying systems about upcoming changes. Each will be described in the following paragraphs and their strengths and weaknesses highlighted.

Multiple Bills of Materials. Apart from the work involved in loading additional bills of materials to the files, this is the simplest kind of effectivity system. It may be mandated by the type of change or as a result of lot traceability demanded by a government agency.

With two completely separate bills of materials, production schedules can call for the old bill of material up to the effectivity date of the change and switch to the new one after that. The old bill of materials can be deleted after the effectivity date is past and retained in a history file for spare parts support purposes.

FIGURE 38

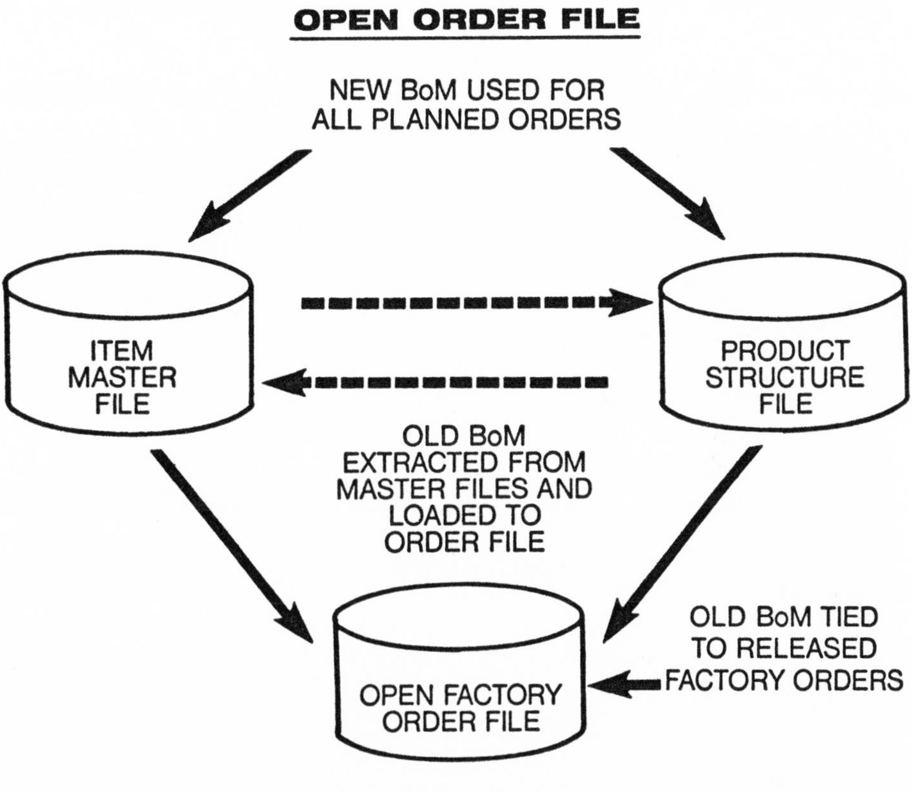

OPEN ORDER FILE

NEW BoM USED FOR
ALL PLANNED ORDERS

ITEM
MASTER
FILE

PRODUCT
STRUCTURE
FILE

OLD BoM
EXTRACTED FROM
MASTER FILES AND
LOADED TO
ORDER FILE

OPEN FACTORY
ORDER FILE

OLD BoM TIED
TO RELEASED
FACTORY ORDERS

A slight variation is when an open order or requirements file exists for each factory production lot. This is simply an extraction of information from the bills of materials and routing files that shows the specific configuration of each lot in process. If this facility is available, the old bills of materials can be loaded on the open order file for all production orders up to the new design implementation date. It can be deleted from the normal bills of materials files which now contain only the new bills of materials.

This latter approach demands specific features within the material control system to get the planning and scheduling of old and new materials done correctly. First, the system must recognize the differences between scheduled orders with their bills of materials defined now on the open order file, and planned orders where the bills of materials are resident on the product structure and item master files. The relationship is shown in Fig. 38.

Second, the system must either contain time phased allocations or explode scheduled orders to get requirements for lower level components

FIGURE 39

EFFECTIVITY DATES

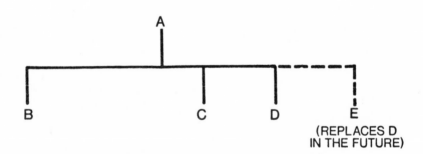

PRODUCT STRUCTURES

Relationship	Effectivity Status	Effectivity Date	Eng'g Change No.
A – B	BUILD	—	—
A – C	BUILD	—	—
A – D	FUTURE DELETE	WEEK 15	49765
A – E	FUTURE ADD	WEEK 15	49765

into the right time slot. Another alternative is the system must have firm planned orders and allow their bills of materials to be defined on the open order file. Because the orders are planned, requirements for components will be placed in the right time slot using normal material requirements planning logic.

Without one of these features, under "normal" system control, releasing orders reserves components immediately, destroying knowledge of when they are really required, the main reason for using the bills of materials for planning and scheduling in the first place.

Effectivity dates. These are simply a way of having old and new structures on the same bills of materials file at the same time. The effectivity date is the clue that allows correct planning of the phase-out of old items and phase-in of new. This is shown in Fig. 39.

Part D is the old item that must be deleted in the future. Part E is its replacement. The bill of materials contains both items, even though one or the other is redundant. A code is used to inform the system that one item is in a pending delete condition and the other a pending add. With this code in place, all that remains is to decide when the change should take place. This effectivity date is then carried in the product structure file, available for a variety of computer programs.

Establishing effectivity dates should not be thought of as the end to getting changes introduced on time. The date is a forecast, and could be based on old material use up rates, accurate records of good inventories, and new parts availability. Hence, no attempt should be made to automatically change over to the new design on these forecasted dates. Constant monitoring of actual events, preferably manually, should be done to verify the date is valid or change it if not. A listing from the product structure files in date order of change can assist in reviewing the close-in changes more aggressively as their upcoming effectivity dates approach. The dates help the planning process but execution still needs management attention. Once the change has been implemented, the old product structure record should be deleted from the working files and the bill of materials retained for historical purposes.

It is possible to use two dates in an effectivity system, a start date and a stop date. These are particularly helpful for temporary deviations, especially those caused by predictable interruptions in supply. Of course, this doubles the complexity of executing the change, forcing even tighter monitoring and control of the dates.

Sometimes changes must be made to several parts simultaneously, which can be very involved and affect both parts and sub-assemblies. One way of tieing these related changes together is to use the Engineering Change Number that authorized the change. If it is possible to have multiple changes on one engineering change document, some that relate and others that do not, then a suffix to the engineering change number that uniquely identifies related changes can be used. This means carrying the change number in the computer files also, as shown in Fig. 39. This additional piece of data shows clearly which items must all be changed at the same time, and hence, must have the same effectivity date.

A modification to the date change technique is called "block changes". This technique forces most changes to a product to occur at a given point in time. It is used by the automotive industry where most changes occur at the year-end model changeover. But it should receive much wider acceptance. The costs of many small changes occurring throughout the year on a company's product line can be reduced dramatically by limiting changes to certain times of the year on each product. Only mandatory changes, what the automotive industry calls "Ralph Nader" changes, should be allowed outside of these timing constraints. The benefits of block changes are parts lists that are up to date and simple service parts history, again, for example, the automotive industry where the model and year are all that are necessary to define needed repair parts. Accurate, stable costs can be calculated for valid profit and margin statements. History retention is much easier under block changes, again the model and year bill of materials is all that is needed. And the ability to procure materials and parts, and produce products with a stable bill of materials reaps untold benefits in less material shortages and higher efficiencies.

One engineering department that implemented block changes also found their engineers' time better utilized. Previously, each engineer was assigned specific products and he released changes throughout the year as he saw fit. Under block changes, the engineers were reorganized so all worked on one product at one time to meet the block change implementation date. The design was then "frozen" and the project team assigned a new product and new effectivity date. The productivity of the engineering group working as a team on a product by product basis rather than as individuals by product line paid excellent dividends in getting better designs and more productive use of the engineer's time.

Effectivity quantity. Many times, changes are to be introduced when all the old parts or materials are used up, or at a given number of old items, possibly set as the remainder needed for spare parts support. This seems like a very straightforward way of setting change effectivity but in practice is very difficult. As a general rule, it is much wiser to use effectivity dates, the date set by when the material runs out. Effectivity dates are a straightforward approach that handles all effectivity problems. Effectivity quantity only handles a few isolated cases and is usually not worth the bother.

There are two ways effectivity quantity can be done. The best way is to carry redundant structures as shown in Fig. 39 for effectivity dates. A separate engineering change file links together parts D and E, E to replace D. After all requirements have been posted to both D and E, part number D's requirements are netted against its on-hand inventory and a run out date calculated. All future requirements for D are deleted. The calculated run out date is then transferred to part E and all requirements up to this point deleted. The netting for E can now start and replenishment orders planned.

Another way to control the use of quantities is to use the approach shown in Fig. 40. Here the new item E is made a component of the old item, D. From a theoretical standpoint, and for simple changes it is practical too, this is a valid way of using quantity to control change effectivity. A number of other changes must also occur though, at the same time. First, the lot sizing rule on the old item must be set to lot-for-lot (discrete), or in other words an absence of lot sizing. The lead time on the old item must be set to zero and its safety stock set to the effectivity quantity. With this arrangement, the requirements for D will be netted against its inventory and when the availability reaches zero its requirements become planned orders exploded into requirements for E. After the change has been implemented, the bill of materials must be maintained to link part number E directly to A and to drop out both the A to D and D to E linkages.

FIGURE 40

EFFECTIVITY QUANTITY

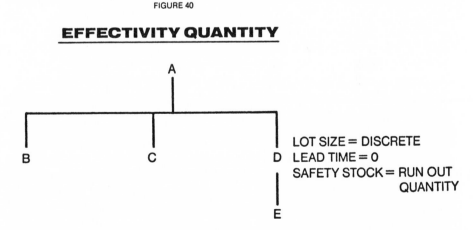

LOT SIZE = DISCRETE
LEAD TIME = 0
SAFETY STOCK = RUN OUT QUANTITY

The drawback with this technique is the amount of information required to be changed on the old and new parts, both before and after the change has been implemented. It is a difficult technique to use with multiple deletions and additions and causes some disruption if the bills of materials have other uses. For instance, costing this bill of materials results in funny numbers with no way of predicting variances between the old and the new. Some computer programs reject this arrangement if D is a purchased item, as they have an edit, mentioned in Chapter 8, that a purchased item cannot have a bill of materials. So another change is required to code D as a manufactured part to get around this objection.

Pick lists for the parent item are also invalid with effectivity quantity. And the worst problem may be that the change is only understood by a few people. The logic of use up the old and then replace with the new sounds straightforward until the mathematics and variety of changes involved are considered. If five parts are to be deleted and replaced simultaneously in an assembly, which part is the controlling item and how are all these structures linked together? And is "use up till all gone" a frequent change or is the availability of new materials, tooling or components the usual limitation? If it is, then dates are the best effectivity tool. Effectivity quantity can be a nervous technique, changing implementation dates as schedules are revised, inventory adjustments are made or scrap occurs. Hence, monitoring and reporting of the change implementation date becomes a very real chore.

Serial effectivity. Many companies assign serial numbers to the products they make. This is common in the aircraft industry where airframe, engine, and other key modules are assigned serial numbers before being produced. Changes are then planned, to be introduced at a given serial number, and the system uses serial numbers as they key effectivity point.

This is a feasible tool for low-volume and well-controlled production, but it is still not easy. It is not good for high-volume, flexible manufacturing because the serial numbers predicted ahead of time fall out of sequence as schedules are revised. Hence it is difficult to coordinate on the factory floor the actual implementation of the change.

Where feasible, serial numbers similar to effectivity dates mentioned earlier are used. The planning system keys off the serial number to establish when to switch requirements from the old part to the new. But as simple as this sounds, it is not that easy to actually coordinate changes to a given serial number, and rarely is it necessary. The planning system is more complex as it explodes serial numbers down the bill of material to control change, limitations are often placed on lot-sizing decisions at lower levels—especially for common items, to keep the serial number track—and extra sales or unexpected scrapping of the old part can force more old parts to be made to meet a given unit's serial number. And instead of making more old parts, the change could be made—and is often desirable to be made—at an earlier serial number. But the system automatically orders the old part.

There are few good reasons to plan effectivity by serial numbers. Contrary to many beliefs, military procurement regulations rarely require *planning* of change by serial number. However, they do require for many products *recording* of change by serial number. As products are made and serial numbers assigned, the specific configurations of the product as built must be recorded and linked to the serial number. For example, a change was effective starting at serial number 12345 or effective for serial numbers 56789 through 67890. Under this scenario, the actual planning of the change can be through effectivity dates or effectivity quantity, a much simpler proposition.

Cost Allocation

Many people feel that worrying about the charges for engineering changes is a waste of time and effort as the changes will be made anyway. This is simply not true. If charges are not made to specific accounts the costs will end up in the nebulous categories of manufacturing variance, tool budget over-runs, and of course the year end inventory write-off. The groups responsible for these accounts become victims of events they cannot control, as they are being measured without the authority to manage the results. Allocating the costs out of these accounts into specific budgets for each function makes the costs of change visible and manageable.

For changes demanded by the customer, wherever possible all costs should be charged directly to him. It is amazing how few companies do this well. In most cases, assuming the charges are documented, the customer will accept the bill. Failure to notify him is simply a loss of profits. Where the customer will not pay for the change, the sales department is often charged, defining the costs as part of the costs of selling to this customer. Again, once these charges show up on the .sales budgets, salesmen become much more aggressive at recovering all or part of the costs of the change, with a consequent increase in profits.

For mandatory or as-soon-as-possible changes that are not customer caused, many companies assign all change related costs to the designers. This may be a little harsh when government regulations are changed but in most cases these are proposed and suggested way ahead of the actual implementation date and some even have a future date of effectivity. Failure of designers to be aware of these proposed changes is a failure of their function, so they should bear the costs. By assigning all costs of quick changes, the most expensive kind, to the designers, they can be made to realize how their failures affect the company's financial performance. Some companies have seen a dramatic reduction of mandatory changes with this charging procedure, simply because of the greater awareness it creates, with a consequent reduction in out-of-pocket costs.

For all other changes, the charges should be allocated to the causing party. There is often disagreement here as to the correct reason for the change and hence who should be charged. In some cases, purchasing or quality control can be charged for the change, especially if the cause is because the vendor they selected cannot produce the item within specification. Similarly, manufacturing can also be charged if the process they developed does not produce an acceptable product.

One of the best ways to decide the allocation is through an independent function such as accounting. Since accounting is often a member of the Engineering Change Review Team, allocation becomes one of their regular duties. As a general rule, accounting should always be a member of the review team. Their focus on cost/benefit numbers will help assure only profitable changes are implemented and that costs are recovered or allocated to the source wherever possible.

Some companies do not like this spreading of costs and hence allocate them to one function, for example, engineering or production and inventory control. If engineering is assigned the costs, they will become resistant to making any changes unless they benefit. If production and inventory control is assigned the costs, they will tend to delay implementation until the last item is used up with zero obsolescence. Hence, it may be better simply to accumulate all the change costs in an account chargeable to the review board, to avoid the parochial reflexes mentioned above. But only do so after full recognition that the costs will be less managed by the board than when assigned to operating budgets.

History

Almost all companies need to record the design of their products, either for spare parts support, field modification, warranty claims or liability protection. The engineering change process should include this vital activity.

There are a variety of ways of recording history. One is to leave the data on the computer disk files tagged as inactive, which is expensive at the moment, but prices for disk storage are dropping fast. Another is to transfer the data to magnetic tape files, a much cheaper storage medium but also less accessible. A third way is to convert the data to microfilm. On microfilm the data is condensed but also quickly accessible, especially with a good indexing method indicating the engineering change number, date of change, parent number and component number changed. Still another way is with paper records filed in books and cross indexed.

Whatever method is chosen, it is important to think through the reasons for storage and the need for access. Far too many companies store too much or too little historical data about their bills of materials and other companies know they have the data but cannot find it easily. A well thought out historical retention and retrieval system can pay enormous dividends in supporting customers, shipping the right spare parts on time and generally providing an aura of control and dependability to the field.

Accuracy

Every engineering change is a potential error in the records. The next chapter is devoted to accuracy of bills of materials. Pull every trick in the book to audit the quality of data entering the system. Bills of materials are one of the foundations of a manufacturing company. Don't destroy it by paying only lip service to the quality of data the foundation needs.

8 Accuracy

The additional uses for bills of materials in today's modern manufacturing plants have generated extreme pressures for accuracy. The concept of one set of data used by all functions is a radical departure from the past, when several manual bills of materials existed in a plant, all somewhat different for a variety of reasons, sometimes simply because of errors. Now, with one set of data in a computer, manual over-rides to compensate for errors are not possible. Detailed planning, scheduling, costing and kitting functions are performed automatically, with little or no human intervention. Hence, this data must be entered accurately and maintained accurately through all the changes and modifications most products undergo. Because of the volume of data involved, a specific, conscious effort is needed to get and keep high levels of accuracy. Without it, significant errors creep in and destroy the formal system's functions, inviting the informal, fire fighting methods of the past to return. The company's financial performance and its ability to compete in the marketplace are diminished as a result.

Logic Edits

A large number of logical relationships exist between item master and product structure information that can be tested to ensure accuracy in some of the input information. One test is to check that an item master record exists for all items loaded into the product structure file. Failure to find one results in rejection of this product structure linkage.

Another test checks for an item source coded "purchased" that is also a parent of lower level parts. In most cases this indicates an error, either in the coding of the item as purchased or in the fact it has product structure linkages. This is not always true as some companies engineer a product, or a segment of the product, but yet still purchase this from another supplier. A good example is in aircraft manufacture. The major contractor designs an item but segments are purchased from subcontractors. The major contractor needs the bills of materials for product definition, yet the product is coded purchased. Some companies also sell service parts to repair major items they have purchased, which can also cause a purchased item with a bill of materials to be valid. However, these exceptions are rare, hence the few items that should be coded purchased yet also have product structures can be identified and eliminated from this test.

Similarly, an item that is coded manufactured but has no product structure linkages probably also signifies an error. An exception is when one item is a by-product of another and hence does not need any additional material to manufacture it. An example is a disk and ring flame-cut out of the same steel plate. When manufacturing rings, the disk is created automatically and hence no additional material is required for the disk. It *is* manufactured but should have no lower level material linkages.

An interesting control problem, both physical and financial, develops in this situation. As the disk is manufactured with no additional labor or material than is required for making the ring, what costs should be applied to the disk? If set at zero, then the ring carries the total cost which is distributed unevenly if the two parts are used on different products. If an attempt is made to link material and labor to the disk using bills of materials and routings, then, when planning material and capacity, some erroneous duplication of demands will occur. And it gets even more confusing if either disks or rings can be scrapped during subsequent manufacturing steps or if the usage of these two in their respective products is uneven.

If more rings than disks are needed, then extra disks will accumulate. If a cost is applied to disks, then inventories will grow and will have to be written off the books when some are scrapped, even though in essence they were "free". If more disks than rings are needed, then a bill of materials and routing describing how to make disks has to be created, which is only used to make disks additional to those not made as a by-product of producing rings. Informing the planning and control systems when to use this alternative information and when to ignore it, both physically and financially, is a logical nightmare. The best solution is a compromise between a theoretically correct answer and what works adequately for all functions, and often means significant manual intervention.

Another example of a manufactured item with no lower level components was already mentioned in Chapter 4. It occurs in a company that manufactures a product from castings, and the company has its own foundry. In this case, the rough casting is manufactured but it is unlikely the materials to make the casting, such as pig iron and alloying elements, are linked in a bill of materials to the rough casting. This again is a valid exception. Some systems use additional source coding to identify these exceptions to establish a tight control over when items should or should not have product structures. This is a good idea when such occurrences are frequent enough that manual overrides become cumbersome.

Units of Measure

Another good edit is to check that the item master unit of measure matches the unit of measure the engineer needs when he writes the product structure linkages. For example, tape is purchased and costed in rolls, hence this is its unit of measure on the item master file. An engineer requires three inches of tape for a particular application. If the input document to load the product structure file does not have any unit of measure field on it, then the engineer will write down "quantity 3", and the part number for *rolls* of tape. The bill of materials now calls for three full rolls when the engineer means only three inches. Any time a quantity is written on a document it should always be followed by the unit of measure, allowing a cross check between the standard carried in the item master and what was written down. In the previous example, if the engineer had written "quantity 3 inches", this could have been checked against the item master unit of measure and rejected.

Insisting a unit of measure be written down every time a quantity is written on a transaction, and that this unit of measure be checked against the standard in the item master file, is a good rule for documents other than bills of materials. Stories abound of large inventory discrepancies being caused by invalid units of measure, such as transacting 3 *drums* of oil rather than 3 *gallons,* 10,000 *boxes* of staples rather than 10,000 *staples,* and 18 *rolls* of wire rather than 18 *feet.* Purchase orders, receiving documents, stores transactions, sales orders, and any other transaction that carries a quantity should all demand a unit of measure. This will help prevent many computerized inventory and costing errors because item masters are defined with one standard unit of measure but the transaction quantity is for another.

Some companies build conversion rules into their systems to change procurement units of measure into bills of materials units of measure. A good example is the buying of steel by the pound when the bills of materials use feet. Be careful of conversion rules. For example, the commercial tolerances on steel tubing are high and the weight to length ratio is highly variable. One thousand pounds of tubing is not always the same length. It depends on the tolerances in the particular run of steel. And it is *feet* of tubing that makes parts, not pounds. Whenever possible, use the same unit of measure for procurement, stocking and bills of materials, opting for the manufacturing unit of measure if feasible. Don't be tempted into the "easy" way out by using mathematical conversion rules.

Wherever possible, additional edits should be developed to identify errors in the logical relationships between item master and product structure data, as well as the presence or absence of information. Some products have unique characteristics that can be built into such edit routines to detect errors. Let your imagination develop the rules, then implement these into the standard maintenance programs. This will be the first line of defense against erroneous information in the system.

Use the Data

The edits mentioned previously simply check logical relationships between two sets of data. They do nothing to check the validity of the information. A number of other techniques are available to check the quality of the data. One of the best ways is to use a standard costing program to "roll-up" the costs of a product, keeping purchased material costs separate from labor or conversion costs. Standard costing programs use the bills of materials and routings to develop their figures. Comparisons of the material and labor costs between similar products can give interesting results. For example, two engines identical except for the carburetor, should have the same costs other than the differential expected between the two carburetors. This difference can be estimated quite easily. If the standard costs for the two engines do not differ by the estimate, it indicates an error, either within the bills of materials or routings. By keeping material costs separate from conversion costs, the comparison can be made as two separate calculations, material to material, conversion to conversion, to identify the error. Once the general area has been identified, further analysis of costs at lower levels in the bills of materials will eventually locate the error for correction.

The use of standard costs to check bills of materials accuracy is one of the best ways to ensure good data for new products. If they are costed as soon as the bills of materials and routings are available and their costs compared to similar products whose bills of materials have already been checked, major errors can be found before the bills of materials get widespread use. All other ways of detecting errors, other than simple edit or review procedures, identify errors after the bills of materials are in use. Damage has already been done because material has been procured, the factory scheduled and customers promised deliveries, all these actions now invalid because of erroneous data.

Using standard costs as an edit routine requires much faster reactions from purchasing, industrial engineering and accounting departments to provide the necessary costing information on a new product. This is not usually a high priority item with these departments. However, the benefits gained are worth the additional effort. By having material costs rolled up separately from labor costs, an effective test of bills of materials occurs even though routings do not exist for all items. Checking only the material costs against similar products will still check the structure and content of the bills of materials.

Another good way of obtaining accuracy, unfortunately usually after the fact, is to use the bills of materials as a picking document. Extending the quantities of each item on a bill of materials by the run quantity creates a picking document authorizing material to be withdrawn from stores and issued to manufacturing. This information is often checked prior to release into manufacturing by pharmaceutical companies and food processors, where tight control over product manufacture is necessary as a quality control check. If the wrong ingredients are dispensed, then poor quality or rejected material is manufactured, not to mention the dangers if this material is actually sold.

For other companies, if the only material issued to manufacturing is what is on the pick list—no more, no less, this will check whether the production people have adequate materials to produce this production run. If they cannot, an error is present. The documents requisitioning additional materials must now specify the reason. Similarly, if excess materials are delivered and then returned after the production run is completed, the return transaction must also specify the reason. In either case, if it is because of a bill of materials error, this can be verified by engineering and the problem corrected. This requires tight discipline on the movement of materials in and out of the stockrooms to be effective, but can pay off handsomely in error corrections.

Some companies regularly issue a few specially marked bills of materials that are tracked carefully in all departments. The special identification notifies everyone who handles this document to review it for accuracy and clearly mark any errors. All specially identified documents are returned to engineering for evaluation and correction after they have been used. Tracking the sample simply ensures all documents are returned. This is also a good way to get a statistically relevant measure of the overall bill of materials accuracy. Of course, nothing in this procedure precludes errors being recorded and returned to engineering on unmarked bills of materials.

Still another audit is to actually build a product with someone assigned to review the bill of materials accuracy as the product is built. For large, assembled items, this is frequently the only way to get a thorough accuracy check. However, it is a lengthy, time consuming job, and again occurs after all materials have been planned, scheduled, and manufactured to suit what currently exists as documentation.

A slight variation of this approach is to use the returned goods department as the bills of materials checkers. Many companies have returned goods areas where products returned are partially or completely disassembled to ensure they are in good working order before classifying them as new or reconditioned items. If a returned product is to the latest bill of materials revision, then a check of the bill of materials can be done concurrently with the disassembly process. This can also be a check on the quality of product manufacture. Many times quality control finds this test of significant benefit in knowing whether their controls on the manufacturing process are adequate. And it is a "free" way of getting valuable information.

Part Numbers

A discussion on bills of materials accuracy would not be complete without some thoughts on the subject of part numbering, a subject that creates more emotional responses than any other subject within the world of manufacturing control. A complete discussion of part numbers is not possible here, but some comments regarding accuracy are worthwhile mentioning.

Part numbers are the universal communications medium between people, both inside and outside the plant. Customers, salesmen, engineers, purchasing agents, cost accountants, order billing people, factory workers, stock keepers, production schedulers, inventory control people and still others all use the common language of part numbers. The number of transactions that occur utilizing a part number in plants, both verbal and written, ranges from the low five figures per month in small plants into the high six figures per month for large ones. These volumes of transactions demand that the part number be communicated accurately. Error rates as low as 1% cannot be tolerated with this volume of transactions!

Hence, a role for part numbers, at least as important as identifying the product uniquely, is to facilitate accurate communications. A number of tests have been made using letter and number combinations, letters alone and numbers alone, to determine the most accurate system for people to use. Optical scanning equipment is being used more and more to read data so the same tests have been applied to this equipment. All tests point to numbers alone as being more easily identifiable with far less chance of error. With mixed alphabetic and numeric characters, G and 6, 5 and S, B and 8, Z and 2, I and 1, U and V, are all easily mistaken. When speaking, again alphabetic characters are easily mistaken, M and N, K and J, P, B, D, and E, for instance.

The companies who handle millions of transactions a month, for example, Exxon, Sears, or American Express, use numeric characters only for credit card identification. Any alphabetic characters on the card are simply for informational purposes and are not part of the credit card number. Tests have also shown that smaller numbers are easier to write and remember accurately. Hence, the ideal part number is all numeric with as few characters as possible.

Six numeric characters can identify uniquely one million items, more than enough for most companies. But to get one million items identified with only six characters means that no character position can have meaning assigned to it, in other words, a nonsignificant number. Many companies use a significant numbering system, which by definition means the part number must be longer. The serious penalty of more characters in the part number is more inaccuracy when transcribing this information. It is rare that building significance into the number is worth this degradation of accuracy.

An interesting systems check can be built easily into a numeric part number called a "check digit". This is simply a mathematical calculation based on the numbers and their relative positions. A numeric part number, six digits long, with a check digit, will prevent at least 95% of all transposition errors with part numbers, the largest single cause of problems. The large credit card companies like Exxon, Sears, and American Express, all have a check digit at the end of their credit card number. Most banks have check digits as part of their account numbers. Computer programs or data entry devices can be programmed to mathematically calculate the check digit any time a part number is entered, and to compare this to the one at the end of the part number. If they do not match, an error has occurred, needing correction. This test can be done when bills of materials are being loaded into a file originally and when any corrections or modifications are made.

Significance in a part number is usually only necessary when using manual systems; the significance allows data to be manually sorted easily. However, in today's world of computers, sorting can occur quickly using separate sorting codes, splitting the old significant numbers into the significant and unique identifier portions. The unique identifier becomes a small numeric part number with a check digit for accurate transcription and the significant portion is made a separate part of the item master data. A large number of characters can be assigned to the significant data elements, certainly more than is possible with a significant part number.

This is called a classification, characteristic, or commodity code. Such things as the material the item is made from, an approximate idea of its dimensions, its shape (for example cylindrical, flat or tubular) and type of plating can all be coded. Sorting now occurs not using the part number but using characteristic coding. Designers can use this to search for existing items similar to ones currently being designed, with significant savings of design effort, tooling, and the use of more standardized parts.

Other uses for these codes are to aid in group technology, which has the objective of manufacturing similar shaped products in a production cell rather than with discrete functional work centers. The need for productivity improvements in the face of steadily dropping average run quantities and skilled labor shortages will stimulate this way of manufacturing. The move to more automation will also demand standardized designs wherever possible because of the huge outlays needed for tooling. The ability to select all items in a plant that look similar and have similar manufacturing characteristics will be essential to a company's profitability in the future.

Responsibility Assignment

It is hard to stress too highly the need for accuracy in bills of materials. A constant war against errors and their cause must be waged to get and keep adequate quality levels in this vast amount of data. This is not the place to take shortcuts, neither in the quality of people assigned to maintaining this data nor the computer programs that update the various files of information.

This suggests that the responsibility for accurate bills of materials must be clearly assigned to a group or groups of people and their performance monitored to ensure they are achieving the desired accuracy levels. This is always best accomplished when the responsibility is clearly assigned to one group. When multiple functions have the need and opportunity to maintain the same data, confusion and errors always result.

But which group should have this responsibility of maintaining bills of materials accurately? It could be cost accounting, although they are not usually interested in very up-to-date information, and so will probably lag the needs of the other functions for timely maintenance. It could be material control or manufacturing engineering, and the responsibility frequently does lie with one of these groups, but duplication of information between the designers and these groups will occur. And frequently bills of materials take too much of a manufacturing slant. It could be design engineering, where the data originates, but this group often considers bills of materials as a necessary evil to be finished and passed along to someone else as soon as possible so they can get back to their "important" work of new and improved product designs.

Which group to select depends more on the people responsible for the function and their attitude to bills of materials than on the theoretically correct answer, which is design engineering. Design engineering is the correct group for the job simply because the design of the product and the structure of the bills of materials play such a key role in the success or failure of a business. This is discussed in more detail in Chapter 9. However, if the designers are not willing to accept this responsibility, then another group with a vested interest in accuracy and structure, such as material control, should be chosen.

9   Organization

Bills of materials have been used by companies and manufacturing concerns for many years. Accountants use them for costing, engineers use them to instruct the factory how to build the product, the factory uses them to know what to produce, and quality control uses them to give assurance the product meets specifications. The use of bills of materials for planning procurement of raw materials and purchased components, as well as scheduling the plant, has been a relatively new addition to its list of uses. Significant conflicts have occurred and continue to occur between the traditional users of bills of materials and the formats necessary to support them, and the new users and the formats they need. With bills of materials now seen as the critical skeleton for the total logistics planning process for a company, these new roles have become at least as important as the traditional ones and in many cases the most important to improve a company's profitability.

Changing the Design Engineer's Role

The responsibility normally assigned to design engineers is to design a product that performs a given function for a cost low enough for the item to be profitable in the market place. Provided they meet these objectives, design engineers have fulfilled the responsibility historically assigned to them. However, the design of the product is the largest single contributor to determining the amount of inventory a company must carry to provide a desired level of customer service. Production and inventory control people can only work within the framework of the product design to manage inventories and improve customer service. In the final analysis it is the product design that limits and controls achieving these objectives fully.

This suggests the design engineer's role should be expanded to include not only designing a product to perform a function at a suitable cost, but also to design a product that can be forecast well so it provides high customer service levels at the same time that inventories are low. These additional objectives, if applied today in most plants, would modify substantially the design of many products. For an example, see the discussion of the hoist shaft in the modular bills of materials section of Chapter 6.

The design engineer should be the person actively involved in structuring the bills of materials to suit all its conflicting demands. This is not where the responsibility lies in many companies. The maintenance of the bills of materials, meaning the files of data in a computer, is often done by people other than design engineers. Manufacturing engineers frequently have this responsibility, sometimes the people in production and inventory control have it, and in some cases a completely separate function called data base management performs this function.

Without the design people being actively involved in the problems of predicting the future and how to make a valid master production schedule, the design will always be inadequate to achieve the maximum benefits. This change in organization is discussed at length by Dick Bourke in his excellent book, *Bill of Material, The Key Building Block*. This revised view of the bills of materials and the role of the design engineer will be resisted by many engineering people who believe they are currently working under enough constraints without new ones being added. Getting them to accept these new responsibilities will frequently need direction from top management to make sure this change occurs for the benefit of the corporation in total.

Cooperation and Compromise

With all the demands being placed on bills of materials, it is unlikely that one format will suit all functions perfectly. The need for costing people to see data in a certain way may not exactly coincide with the way the engineers would like to define the product or the way manufacturing would like to see the information. Production and inventory control practitioners and sales people, because of their concern for customer service and low inventories simultaneously, also need the bills of materials formatt d to suit them. Ingenuity by computer software people to retrieve information in a variety of ways can help this conflict considerably. However, there will always be some areas where compromise will be necessary for one bill of materials to serve everybody adequately rather than perfectly.

The objective is to have only one bill of materials in the computer to simplify maintenance, obtain accuracy, and to reduce the data stored. Hence, the bill of materials structure will have to be set-up to support these compromises and make them effective. With the right attitudes from all functions and a clear understanding of the objectives and potential of computerized systems, it is rare that a company cannot end up with one bill of materials that serves all its uses adequately and that all functions support. But this expands the role of the design engineer even further, to include an understanding of the workings of the manufacturing environment and all uses of bills of materials, an understanding many design engineers do not have today.

Management Team and the Bill of Material

As mentioned earlier, the bill of materials is the skeleton all planning activities are built upon. It also plays a key role in the performance of many other duties within manufacturing. This means that managers from all functions should understand the various uses of bills of materials and the need to have them constructed in a form that suits all requirements.

Many managers are not even aware that some of their actions work in opposition to getting a well structured bill of materials and because of this they defeat their own purposes. For example, one company had a financial group concerned about the erosion of profit margins. At their instigation, a value analysis team was organized to review the products and cost reduce them wherever possible. The engineers had originally designed a modular product with a lot of standard components. This meant additional operations or parts were always added even though they were only sometimes used. For instance, additional holes were present in many components that sometimes were covered over and not used. Other components had brackets welded on them to suit a particular option and if this option was not selected then this bracket was redundant.

The value analysis team reviewed the products and quickly saw the redundant operations and parts always included but only sometimes used. They quickly eliminated the redundancy but in so doing had to create many new part numbers to define the larger variety of non-standard components and then non-modular finished products. Based on eliminating the redundancies, significant cost savings were projected.

However, with this wider variety of components and less standardization, predicting the future accurately became impossible. Inventories escalated significantly at the same time as customer service dropped off considerably.

There is no question the standard cost of the product was reduced. However, the gains in product margin were more than offset by the increased inventory and the poorer customer service with increased receivables, freight costs, expediting, customer complaints, and additional indirect people required in the new environment. The savings of direct labor had been transferred to indirect labor and increased overhead expenditures with the end result a less profitable organization than before!

Sales and marketing organizations are extremely interested in customer service. They want to offer the widest variety of products possible with the shortest lead time so all customers get the products they want when they want them. But to achieve this objective, they have to contribute to the design of the product and make sure any of their requests for additional features do not serve a short-term need and hurt the long-term. A request to put a specific new option in the line for a given product has to be weighed against the impact adding this option will have on the bills of materials for existing options. If adding it makes the problem of predicting the future much more difficult, then maybe putting this option in the line is not the correct thing to do. Serious consideration of what products or features customers might select should occur when a new product is being introduced. The more thought that is given to the basic design and the potential option selection the customer will be offered while the product is still in its early design stages, the better the finished design will serve all the needs of the company. Without this attention to a new product introduction, add-on requirements superimposed on the basic design will cause significant problems and result in serving customers poorly.

Engineers are creative people. They want to design a product that is better than the competition, but above all else they want to see "their baby" in production. Sometimes though, their drive to design a better product defeats getting it into production and, even worse, defeats any possibility of giving customers what they need when they need it. "Build a better mousetrap and people will beat a path to your doorstep" is a wonderful saying, but if you don't have the one they want in stock or readily available, it is unlikely that they will be back. This additional need for a "logistically effective" design is not recognized by many engineers.

For example, many unique "state of the art" components and raw materials have lead times of 26 to 60 weeks to procure. It is impossible to predict with any degree of accuracy what products customers will buy over such lead times. So the unique and better design languishes in production, with shortages, high inventories and very upset customers.

A slightly less technologically advanced product using quickly obtainable components could be far more profitable for the business. Advanced technology is often useful to get ahead of the competition and there are some fields where customers will wait for products designed with the latest technology. But a fine line exists between "technologically superior" and "impossible to produce on time". These two factors must be weighed carefully and all unique, long lead time items challenged wherever they appear.

Skeleton for Business Success

The bill of materials is the skeleton for all planning activities in a plant. It will determine whether a factory executes the master production schedule or whether it is always in trouble, giving customers poor service and carrying high inventories.

As suggested in the introduction, some serious dislocation of manufacturing will occur as freight and transportation costs (because of fuel price increases) become a higher percentage of a product's delivered cost. This will cause companies to relocate closer to their markets with smaller plants producing a wide variety of finished products. This has already started in some industries. The task now is how to produce a wide variety of products in small volumes efficiently. The secret lies in the basic design of the product and the way this is specified to the logistical planning system. Companies that realize this and capitalize on it are those that will be successful. Those that fail to make this transition will have productivity, inventory, and customer service problems with poor profits on high capital investments.

As progress is made towards the automated factory of the future, the capital expenditures for the equipment for such a factory will be very high. A counterbalancing reduction of inventories will be needed so the total capital employed remains the same. The productivity gains from such a factory will hold costs in line and allow a company to remain competitive. As the bill of materials is so vital to controlling inventories, it is one of the real opportunities for future manufacturing company successes.

If long lead time items are necessary, they must be made common to a wide variety of end products, what I call a "mushroom" product design. This way the common items can be planned to a product group forecast with the variability added at the last moment. Selective overplanning of the long lead time items can simultaneously guarantee excellent customer service, low inventories, and a factory without shortages.

10 Benefits

The work to evaluate existing bills of materials and restructure them to suit the needs of a manufacturing control system can be significant. Hundreds of man years of work may have gone into the existing designs and layouts. In many cases, even more time has been spent loading these existing bills of materials into a computer to support various company activities. And now another review of these structures may be necessary suggesting significant change to the way they are presently defined. This is in many cases a massive project which must be justified based on predictable and significant tangible and intangible benefits.

Inventories

The largest controllable asset in most manufacturing companies is their inventories. Many times this is equal to one half of the total capital employed. The interest rates charged on money borrowed to finance inventories or the lost opportunity of having money tied up in inventory and not available for other business ventures is a cost to be avoided as much as possible.

Significant reductions in the total inventories of a plant can occur with the right bill of materials structure. One company achieved a 30% reduction in total inventories at the same time they achieved a 30% growth in real units sold, doubling the inventory turn-over and contributing significantly to the improved profitability of the company. While these may be extreme numbers, there is no doubt that the inventories carried by almost every manufacturer in the world could be reduced significantly with better planning systems revolving around a better structured bill of materials.

Customer Service

Most companies have quantified objectives for customer service levels, such as fill a given percentage of the orders received from stock or deliver a percent of the products on time to the customer. It is a rare company that meets these objectives.

One company that produces large machinery has an excellent bill of materials structure and a valid master production schedule. They are meeting their promises to customers 98% of the time. With this enviable customer service level, this company has a significant order backlog compared to its competition, even though they charge a premium for their products. A large part of the success of this company can be attributed to their defining the product correctly.

Productivity

This subject is receiving a lot of attention in the press these days. Many people are looking for ways to improve industrial productivity around the world to combat the ever increasing rate of inflation. Most of the solutions to date revolve around ways of making the product better. New machines, new processes, better standards, better tooling, and worker motivation, are the usual approaches suggested. In most cases these solutions demand more investment in capital equipment to obtain the productivity increase.

However, within the actual operations of a plant, there is a lot of lost motion and wasted activity because materials are not available when needed to suit a given customer's order. This can be a result of bad planning or poor execution of the plans, but it is frequently caused because what was forecast to be sold is not what is actually sold. The resulting shortages are filled by scrambling in the plant with split lots, broken set-ups, poor learning curve effects, and not running jobs in an efficient sequence. Indirect labor is added to handle the confusion, air freight costs go up to get the missing components, and the assembly floor builds the product around the shortages. When the short parts come in sometime later, they add them then, usually inefficiently, rather than assembling them during the normal process. There are many stories of production managers looking for long-armed, left-handed assemblers. They are the only people who can reach where the short part goes! This lost motion and frequent additional activities are always less efficient than making the product correctly the first time. Most assembly foremen will quote a potential 10% increase in productivity for their areas provided all the material is there when they need it. And you know they are "sandbagging". One company achieved a 30% productivity increase and at the same time reduced their total inventories substantially. Most engineering objectives for productivity improvements in a plant are targetted below 5% annually. And significant investments are needed to achieve this goal, not less investment, as with a better planning and scheduling approach. Maybe our whole direction needs to be changed.

A large part of the problem can be solved by improving the ability to create a valid master production schedule for the product and to provide contingency to cover the unknowns. However, as has been demonstrated, this can only be done effectively when the bills of materials have been designed and structured to suit this need. If the product has been designed with a lot of uniqueness with no thought given to predicting the future, then shortages and lost motion will occur. There is no way to get an accurate forecast for a unique product several weeks or months in the future. And no matter what process improvements the engineers make and better machines they buy, without parts and materials available when needed, the targeted improvements will not be realized.

Flexibility in the Marketplace—Stability in the Plant

Many companies feel that the need to react quickly in the marketplace and be stable in the plant are conflicting objectives that cannot be reconciled. This is dead wrong. These objectives can be achieved simultaneously with the right planning process.

The marketplace for almost every product in the world is a dynamically changing arena. People buy what they want when they want it; they don't even bother to read a company's forecast before making their decision! There are only two choices available to react quickly to changing market conditions. One is to have contingency built within the plans to cover the needed changes. The other is to have a plant and its vendors dynamically reactive. Both these options have a cost alternative associated with them. If contingency is built into the plan, some excess inventory will be present. If the factory changes plans frequently, then some confusion will occur, costs will go up, and there could be a build-up of inventory because things that were made to the old plan are no longer required; at the same time, additional parts are needed to meet the new plan.

Generally, it is far more preferable to plan contingency in the master production schedule than to make a plant react quickly. This is not always true as some plants and products can react quickly to the marketplace with little or no cost penalties. However, this probably exists in no more than 5% of manufacturing companies. For the other 95%, changing a plant quickly with the resultant excess inventory and additional costs will almost always be worse than having contingency in the master production schedule. And now with contingency buffering the plant from the customer, schedules can be relatively stable, vendors see a steady demand, and the twin objectives of flexibility and stability can be met at the same time.

A Valid Formal System

The pressures on manufacturing are becoming greater and greater. As the lesser developed countries become industrialized to support their large populations, the pressures around the world for manufacturing efficiency and competitive deliveries will escalate. To combat this, the use of formal, mathematical, and frequently computerized systems will grow. Only with the speed of a computer to adjust all detail plans and disseminate consistent information quickly to a large number of people, will most plants be able to operate at higher levels of output with lower levels of inventory than is currently the norm.

This need for a valid, formal system will force a review of all traditional ways of providing information. One of the most significant that must be evaluated carefully is the bills of materials and whether they support the increased pressures on manufacturing. Only with a well designed, well thought out, well maintained bills of materials system will a company have the valid formal system necessary to compete in tomorrow's competitive world.

Bibliography

"Communications Oriented Production Information and Control System (COPICS)", Volume II, IBM 1972.

"European Sets Up Cost-Saver for U.S. Production—Brisch's Coding System", *Business Week,* March 26, 1960.

ANDREW, C., "Engineering Changes to the Product Structure: Opportunity for MRP Users", *Production and Inventory Management,* 3rd Quarter, pp 76-86, 1975.

BECHTEL, T., "Engineering Change Management: A Complete Definition", APICS Conference Proceedings, Readings in Productivity Improvements, pp. 94-97, 1984.

BEYERS, G., "What—Another Part Numbering System?", *Engineering Graphics,* January, 1976.

BEYERS, G., "The Engineering Change Order System", (Three Part Series), *Engineering Graphics,* May-August, 1976.

BOURKE, R., *Bill of Materials—The Key Building Block.* Pasadena, CA: Bourke & Associates, 1975.

BRACKETT, R., "Engineering Change Order Planning and Control", APICS Conference Proceedings, 1980.

BREIMAN, M. and J. T. CLARK, "Production Control Responsibilities in Effecting Engineering Changes", APICS Bulletin, October, 1960.

BRIDGETTE, R., "Engineering Change Control in a Flow Shop Environment," *Production and Inventory Management,* 3rd Quarter, pp 26-31, 1977.

CAMPBELL, K.L., "Responding to Product Structure Changes in a Net Change MRP", APICS Conference Proceedings, 1976.

CARLSON, J., "Item Identification and Classification in Management Operating Systems", *Production and Inventory Management,* 2nd Quarter, pp 23-32, 1971.

CATTO, J., "Nonsignificant Part-Numbering of Engineering Drawings"; GAUER, R., "The Significance of Nonsignificant Part-Numbers", "Nonsignificant Part-Numbering Systems", (Reprints of 3 articles, original source unknown) IBM.

CARRUTHERS, J.M., "Product Structure Charts: Key to Designing and Controlling Modular Bills of Material", APICS Conference Proceedings, 1976.

DESALVIA, D. and G. GEMMILL, "The PICM as a Change Agent: Some Techniques for Engineering Opinion Changes", APICS Conference Proceedings, 1972.

DIPRIMA, M., "Engineering Change Control: Key Elements for Improving Productivity", APICS Conference Proceedings, pp. 258-260, 1983.

DOSSETT, L., "Engineering Joins the MRP Crusade", APICS Conference Proceedings, pp. 335-340, 1976.

EVERDELL, R., "Planning Bills of Material: Tools for Master Scheduling", APICS Conference Proceedings, pp. 265-268, 1983.

FRANK, D., "Engineering Change: Too Important to Leave to the Engineers", APICS Conference Proceedings, 1980.

FULTON, J.W., "Designing Identification Codes", *Automation,* October, 1964.

GALLAGHER, G. and J. GULLO, "Developing a Closed Loop MRP System— What's In It for the Design Engineer?", *Production & Inventory Management,* 4th Quarter, 1980.

GARWOOD, D., "Stop: Before You Use the Bill Processor", *Production & Inventory Management,* 2nd Quarter, 1970.

GREENE, J., ed., "Product and Process Information", Chapter 5 in *Production and Inventory Control Handbook.* NY: McGraw-Hill, 1970.

GRUMMAN, E.V., "Engineering and Engineering Change as Related to Production Control", APICS Conference Proceedings, 1966.

GUESS, V., "What are the Relationships Between P & IC and Engineering?", APICS Conference Proceedings, 1979.

_____, "The Dual Bill of Material: A New Solution", APICS Conference Proceedings, 1980.

_____, *Engineering: The Missing Link in MRP.* Vanard Lithographers, 1979.

GUNDER, W., "Phantom Assemblies", *Production Engineering,* May, 1980.

HEWITT, P.M., "Tips for Better Parts Numbering", APICS Bulletin, April, 1963.

HOFFMAN, R.F., "Structuring a Product Model Data Base", APICS Conference Proceedings, 1977.

HUGE, E., "Engineering Change Control", APICS Conference Proceedings, pp 81-93, 1977.

JACKSON, J., "To Peg or Not To Peg", APICS Conference Proceedings, 1973.

LANGENWALTER, D.F., "Structuring Complex Products", *Production & Inventory Management,* 4th Quarter, 1976.

LEIBLICH, J. and D. SIMONTON, eds, *Drawing Requirements Manual for Departments of Defense and Commerce.* Santa Ana, CA: Global Engineering Documentation Services, Inc., 1976.

MANTELL, S., "Engineering Changes - A Competitive Requirement", APICS Bulletin, July, 1961.

MATHER, H.F., "Which Comes First, The Bill of Material or Master Production Schedule?", APICS Conference Proceedings, 1980.

_____, "Work the Details or Play the Percentages", George Plossl Educational Services Newsnote #34, 1981.

MERCER, B., "Considerations in Structuring Bills of Material", APICS Conference Proceedings, 1974.

MEYERS, A.F., "Standardize Parts to Cut Inventories, Costs, and Stockouts", *Production & Inventory Management*, July, 1967.

ORLICKY, J., *Material Requirements Planning*. NY: McGraw-Hill, 1974.

ORLICKY, J., G. PLOSSL, and O. WIGHT, "Structuring the Bill of Material for MRP", *Production & Inventory Management*, 4th Quarter, 1972.

PLOSSL, G. and O. WIGHT, "Material Requirements Planning by Computer", APICS Special Report, 1971.

POYSER, J., "Learning to Live with Engineering Changes", *Machine Design*, November 19, 1964.

ROEDING, R., "Manufacturing Change Control System", APICS Conference Proceedings, pp 489-498, 1978.

SAMARAS, T. and F. CZERWINSKI, *Fundamentals of Configuration Management*. NY: John Wiley & Sons, 1974.

SARI, J., *The MPS and the Bill of Material go Hand-in-Hand*. Richard C. Ling, Inc. 1981.

WEINBERG, M., "Manufacturing Control Through Product Design: An Engineering Perspective", APICS Conference Proceedings, pp. 269-272, 1983.

WIGHT, O., *Production and Inventory Management in the Computer Age*, Chapter 4. Boston, MA: CBI Publishing Company, 1974.

Illustrations

Index

Index